'I always want someone to walk into their kitchen and feel like it's their favourite room in the house.'

The deVOL Kitchen

Paul O'Leary

Paul O'Leary co-founded deVOL in 1989 and began specialising in freestanding kitchen furniture. By the late nineties, Paul had become the sole proprietor and continued to focus on producing the highest quality cabinetry that reflected deVOL's affinity with simple Georgian and Victorian furniture. This strong design ethic has attracted clients from around the world to its showrooms in Cotes Mill, London and New York, and won him numerous kitchen and design awards. Paul has been a regular commentator on kitchen design in magazines and national newspapers, as well as on radio and TV, most recently starring in and helping to create deVOL's Emmy-nominated TV series. Paul will forever be a product designer at heart, solving the simplest and most complex of design problems while always considering style, form, function and comfort. His innovative and unique ideas have been key in designing and developing deVOL's furniture ranges and ever-expanding collection of accessories.

Helen Parker

Helen Parker is deVOL's Creative Director. She joined in 2004 as a kitchen designer and by 2011 she had become responsible for deVOL's style, creating one-of-a-kind showrooms, sourcing antiques and gifts and designing new pieces of furniture and accessories. Over the years, she has developed deVOL's look and voice, styling all its beautiful imagery, writing for its brochures and website, and is often featured in national and international press. Recently, Helen has starred in and helped to produce deVOL's Emmy-nominated TV series. Helen's passion and desire to create a special look for deVOL has proved to be the making of this company.

Robin McLellan

Robin began his deVOL career as a placement student and his willingness to turn his hand to anything, passion for period furniture and lifelong interest in carpentry have allowed him to completely transform the way deVOL manufactures its furniture. Since becoming Managing Director in 2011, Robin has introduced state-of-the-art machinery and methods into the workshops, which have enabled deVOL to grow exponentially. Robin has an understanding and love of traditional techniques and never loses sight of the importance of these, but knows just how to use them in a modern way to produce a beautiful product efficiently and accurately. When Robin is not setting up workshops or dealing with the day-to-day business of running deVOL, he can be found in the workshops designing and making prototypes, welding metal or turning wood. He is the force that drives deVOL each and every day.

The deVOL Kitchen

Paul O'Leary   Robin McLellan   Helen Parker

Clarkson Potter/Publishers
New York

Contents

This is us

Paul is the Founder and Director of deVOL,
which he started in 1989 at the age of 25.

If you fail, it's not the end of things

Paul O'Leary

I've always considered myself quite an unremarkable chap. I was over a year younger than my class all the way through school and the youngest sibling of three in my family. I went to a boys' boarding school run by priests, where punishments were harsh and readily meted out. I was fearful of failure and not fitting in and totally relieved when I snuck away for good. I've always told myself that my life really only started at that point. I headed off to art college, where freedom, creativity and girls made life a whole lot more fun for a 17-year-old slip of a lad, still wet behind the ears.

A foundation course in Art and Design is just a taster really. You try a bit of everything: life drawing, photography, sculpture, model making – pretty much anything that's fun. It's the polar opposite of revising for A Levels. The culture is laid back; it's up to you how hard you try, and nobody's going to beat you with a cane for talking out of turn.

It was like coming out of prison and going to summer camp. I loved every project they set us, but I also saw more talented people all around me. They seemed so much freer at expressing themselves. I don't really blame myself for not doing a great deal of work. College serves many purposes, and I just needed to live a little, do a lot of growing up and figure out who I was.

Having too much fun was bound to end in failure, and it didn't take too long to find that out. Before the year was done, my mates were being accepted for degree courses around the country, while I continued to drag my meagre portfolio around second-rate colleges to no avail. It was a sorry day when I said goodbye to the lovely friends I'd made and left our halls of residence with nothing lined up for next year. Moving back to Mum and Dad's and getting a job in a factory was the bitterest pill, but maybe just the motivation I needed.

I worked in an engineering firm that made huge electrical switchboards for power stations. I was drilling copper bars and bolting down relays alongside dozens of other teenagers. They would go out at the weekend and spend all their money on lager and fruit machines, without a thought of what else they could be doing. But I'd seen the promised land and I wanted to get back there.

If my portfolio wasn't good enough, then I'd have to retake my A Levels and get into university to do a design course. I gave up my job, left home and bunked down on my college friends' sofas. I worked in temping agencies and spent a year doing evening classes with a focus I'd never known before. Instead of being shushed, I was doing the shushing. All the same, I had no idea whether this renewed effort would be enough.

I'll never forget the day I got my results though. I was just getting over glandular fever and was cycling across Ireland with my girlfriend, Jane, who was a jewellery student. I slotted my 10p pieces into a red phone box somewhere near Tipperary and listened to my dad read out my results. I'd never been so happy. I had exceeded all expectations and finally I was in. It was the first little something I could actually feel proud about.

The degree course in Industrial Design at Loughborough University was perfect for me. I'm not an artist and I'm not an engineer. I'm somewhere in between, and as it turns out, that's not a bad place to be. If ever there was a course made for a skill set that wasn't easily identifiable, this was it. Week one: take a picture of the department from the air, by Friday! The sort of brief that makes you just shrug your shoulders and look blankly around you. Groups formed. What about a kite, a box kite? We'll need balsa wood sticks, or bamboo. We'll need polythene or fabric. Is there a fabric stall on the market? We had ideas and we had to get stuck in because on the next bench somebody was way ahead of us. Week two: make a car that can travel the furthest using this rubber band. And while we pondered each

new problem, we had hands-on experience using lathes and milling machines, learning about vacuum forming and injection moulding.

It was three years of learning how to solve problems, and I didn't just apply those newfound skills to coursework. One of my most pressing problems was money, or my complete lack of it. Students lived in slums in those days, with cling film on the windows and flea powder around the carpet. Clothes were from charity shops, and we ate beans and tinned tomatoes to afford a night out. With begged-for overdrafts creeping higher and bank managers' 'Nos' becoming ever more stern, it was time to get resourceful.

So I hitched rides and earned cash pavement-drawing or gathering mistletoe for free in France and selling it on the streets, in the run-up to Christmas, back in England. By a determination that I'll never figure out, with a £1,600 overdraft and no job, I managed to buy a house. Still in my second year at university, I had become quite the problem solver, and no problem was too big. I set my sights on an eight-bedroom house that I would let out to students to pay the mortgage. Of course, the bank manager said no, over and over, but I phoned him every Monday morning at five past nine for two months and asked him to change his mind. One day, in a moment of madness, he did! When I turned up on my bicycle to this four-storey Victorian villa, the other students gathered at the door asked if I was here to look at the house as well. I said 'No, I'm the landlord!' Looking back, that was remarkable indeed, and it set me up for many attempts at business, all of which ended in failure, but as I've found out, failure is quite the cathartic experience.

Every failure tells its own story, and to an enquiring mind, it's easy to see what went wrong after the event. The most important lesson of all was the realisation that failure is not the end of things. For me, failure became nothing more than a train coming to a halt at the station. It's not necessarily the end of the line, you just have a choice to make.

A young Paul just at the beginning of his journey into business.

Stay on, get off, take another train – there are lots of options. When the train pulls in, there's time to reconsider and recognise what's important. So when I lost the house, I was OK with that, and being broke was something I was used to. The house was gone, but so was the mortgage. I had no kids and I was young, so I could just go again. There really wasn't much to get upset about. Especially because I had gained such a lot. I was wiser, more canny and less naive, my eyes wider open, more awake to the ways of the world.

Each failure made me more resilient and even more determined. I thought, how hard can it be? I can do this. I soaked up advice like a sponge, always asking anyone who ran their own show what made it tick. In the end the answers are simple, business is simple, success is simple, and you look back and wonder how it took you so long to see just how simple it really is.

This is a book about kitchens and design, and it's also about deVOL, which is quite a remarkable story. We came from nowhere, the three of us, but each of us has something unique that stems from our childhood and the things that interested us. We are all shaped by experience and it's the challenges that really wake you up and make you into the somebody you become.

The three of us bring different things to the table, each of them essential, and we also recognise that we can't do it alone. We each lack what the others have, so we pull together on different ropes, but all in the right direction.

For many years, we were working from a very unremarkable brick shed on an industrial estate. Your premises say a lot about your business, and we needed to find a place that would really put us on the map and set us apart from every other local joinery shop. That's when we found Cotes Mill; the great white elephant, a forgotten gem on the River Soar where it had been perched for over a thousand years. What seemed at first like an impossible dream soon became our greatest and most rewarding adventure.

Whenever I look at our sales chart for that period, I call it the Cotes Mill effect. Orders grew and the calibre of kitchens moved up a notch too. It gave us the confidence to open a shop in London. It's a big step for a company from the Shires to open up in the Big Smoke. It was a risk, it meant lots more overheads and we had no idea if it would work. But my hunches seemed to be paying off; so onwards and upwards – we were on a roll. This time we bought a lovely listed Georgian house in Clerkenwell and converted it into another showroom. We were blown away by how well it was received, and before long we had some really big names walking through our door; I mean like 'Oh-my-God-guess-who-walked-into-the-shop-today?' type people.

Below: The Classic Millhouse Kitchen at Cotes Mill, white cupboards with porcelain pendants and a Carrara marble sink. Right: Cotes Mill sits on the River Soar in Leicestershire.

Our first shop in London sits on the corner of Tysoe Street and Exmouth Market in Clerkenwell, London.

Left: Our second London shop can be found on St John's Square, right in the heart of Clerkenwell.

Right: The showroom has three floors of kitchen displays, antiques and gifts.

Below: Classic English cupboards, painted in our exclusive Clerkenwell Blue, with our special handmade Emerald Green wall tiles.

So, what does a boy who was very familiar with failure do when everything seems to be going right? Think of the most ridiculous next step and just do it, without a second thought.

Before I knew it, I was gliding down Broadway on Google Maps Street View, checking out the nicest cobbled streets where deVOL might find a new home. Helen designed the most beautiful interior for our new place on Bond Street in Manhattan,

and after several months of battling with planning regulations and visa applications, we were ready for the most glorious opening night.

If I'd ever wondered whether being in the right place at the right time was really a thing, the eve of our opening proved that serendipity does actually change lives. In walked Chip and Joanna Gaines, who offered us a TV series. We had no idea who they were. We nearly said no.

Opposite: deVOL's first showroom in the States can be found on Bond Street, in the East Village, Manhattan.
Above: Inside Bond Street, this part of the showroom features our Classic English cupboards.

Now deVOL has become a thing. I read some reviews about our series *For the Love of Kitchens* and someone said, 'I was so sick of deVOL mania in the States until I watched their show, and then I got it.' I mean, deVOL mania, really? What is it about deVOL that makes people take notice of little old us? How do we find ourselves with an invitation to attend an Emmy nomination?

How on earth did that all happen? Honestly, if you had seen where we came from, and not that long ago, you would think it completely impossible. But if there's just one thing that made the difference, that drove us forward when we could have – maybe should have – given up or rested on our laurels, it's the total absence of one thing: fear of failure.

Below: First airing in 2021, each episode follows a kitchen project from start to finish and the day-to-day work of the designers & makers at Cotes Mill. Opposite: A small but bold cottage kitchen in County Durham, one of the many projects featured on 'For the Love of Kitchens'.

Helen has been the Creative Director at deVOL since 2011 and has been instrumental in developing the brand into what it is today.

I have found a purpose

Helen Parker

I am slightly apprehensive about the first words I put on this page. I am not a writer, but then again, I am not a designer, if qualifications are anything to go by. I have so much to say and so much to be grateful for. I feel almost too lucky, but not eloquent enough, quite yet, to tackle writing those important words. Those stories will come, though. They absolutely have to if my story and the part I play at deVOL is to make any sort of sense. I hope my journey and the reason I now work at deVOL will be inspiring. Even more, I hope it will be exciting to know that miracles really do happen, people can be sent to save you. It always happens to other people doesn't it, a bit like winning the lottery? I still pinch myself, eighteen years on, that I actually did win a kind of lottery without even buying a ticket!

I am the kind of person who lies awake at night, head full of ideas for the next day, then decides that maybe those ideas were silly or too difficult. I am not naturally ambitious, and I am not particularly focused or driven, but I have found a purpose, a role, a job that is so me, it makes me all those things. I am always embarrassed to say I am a designer, as that sounds like a title, or a profession that requires studying and passing exams and knowing trade secrets. That's not how I came to do this job. I look back on past photoshoots, showroom displays and creations over my time at deVOL and wonder if I will be able to keep pulling it off again and again. Is being creative a given, or can it suddenly fail you? That's a question I don't like to think about. Maybe a true designer doesn't need to worry or maybe we are all just winging it. Whatever the answer is, I call myself a person who likes to play around with ideas and come up with a room or an object that creates an emotion.

People now message me and ask for advice or tips on how to design their kitchen or their home and I am always reticent to reply – not because I am being unhelpful, but because I have a way and it doesn't follow a clear sense or reason. I take such a long time to think about how I want something to end up. I look at and consider everything, every little detail, every option and every possibility before I will put pencil to plan. So, for me to help someone else, I need too much information to give a quick response. If I'm going to do something, it has to be thought about carefully and for a good length of time.

Helen's kitchen is composed of a short Classic sink run, painted in black, and an assortment of vintage pieces, deVOL accessories and a matching black Lacanche range cooker.

Then there is the feeling that I might have to compromise on my design to give the customer what they want. For me, design is about not compromising, because compromise spoils a look. These are harsh words, I know, and I have spent many years before I got to thinking this way, designing other people's kitchens and allowing compromise while still completely loving the process and the finished result.

There is a caveat to compromise, though. I have a reluctance to alter certain things, and this can be a nuisance for an expectant customer if they are keen to knock stuff down and create new spaces. I am always thinking about making something beautiful, but it is even more exciting if this means transforming something that already exists rather than starting from scratch. I love nothing more than working around things that are already there, and that can be a big compromise. Say you have a Victorian house with a rather long, thin kitchen, but you want a wide kitchen. I like the idea of making the long, thin kitchen look beautiful, because it is part of the original house and it is meant to be that way, but that is a compromise – or at least it can be if you choose to look at it that way. Imagine a big, wide kitchen with huge glass doors out onto the patio, wouldn't life be so much better? Yes, that might be great, but it also might be nice to have a long, thin kitchen and a beautiful wooden back door. It might just be even better.

People spend their lives changing things in their homes, more so now than ever before. Sometimes it is life-changing and essential but sometimes it is not. We have this notion today that life will be better or easier or more fun if we have a bigger room or a wider door or a different-shaped house! In my own experience, being in a beautiful room that isn't the perfect shape and size but is full of character and soul, and has maybe even given you a few sleepless nights, is truly life-changing.

I am always smitten by an old kitchen, the kind you see on Instagram in an Ibizan farmhouse or an East London terrace. No walls knocked down, an original sink, a rickety kitchen table, but maybe a fabulous new piece of art on the wall, big and bold and unique. This, for me, is truly inspirational. It is preserving well-made things that have survived for many years but adding your own touches of style and modernity.

I look at design as a whole. I don't consider each aspect of a kitchen, its function, its practicality or its use, in isolation. I imagine a finished room from the very beginning. I imagine the emotion I want it to create and think about how I can achieve that look while knowing the need for function and practicality. I go backwards, I suppose. I start with a completed vision, right down to a geranium on the kitchen table, and I work backwards, never giving up on the geranium but trying not to give up on the cooker or the sink either. So, you see, it may come across as a little lazy when I answer a customer's quick style question by suggesting a geranium on the kitchen table instead of where to locate the all-important wine fridge or food processor. But it's the way I do it. It isn't the best way or the right way or a proven method. It is just me.

Since I was a child, the kitchen has always been the place where everything happened. We didn't have a television that we would sit around. It was hidden behind a large armchair in the drawing room and was only allowed to be turned on for special requests. *Top of the Pops* on Christmas Day was one of those occasions. Instead, we gathered in the kitchen. I would draw, my grandma would sit close to the Aga and the dogs would lie in front of it. It was an old-style Aga that required coal twice a day to keep it hot. Above the Aga on the high ceiling was a laundry maid, always laden with drying clothes. Everything that mattered happened around the table. My father had what is probably now seen as quite an avant-garde taste in food.

Accessories can make all the difference! Classic English cupboards, paired with a magnificent marble sink, aged brass taps, handcrafted fittings and our teal Lace Market wall tiles.

He would eat raw tripe with vinegar and chicory. He would open cans of strange fish in oil or brine and have cheese with his Eccles cake. He would marvel at the taste of a simple tomato. I think this early adventure into food was all part of the reason I love to cook. It all connects, the kitchen and the family and the enjoyment of eating together. There is nothing that leaves you feeling as good as eating together.

I have never given the kitchen such adulation until now, but suddenly, writing this book, I can see how it has been the centre of so much, if not all, of my life. Bringing up my children, Max and Zoë, was something very special to me and it centred around the kitchen. From when they were babies, I decided I would always try to make them good food. I felt comfortable in the kitchen with them by my side and the smell of something cooking. I began to see the importance of spending time preparing ingredients together or just having them there watching the goings-on. No pressure to entertain them, just a comforting clatter that meant home and family and warmth. When times got tough, the kitchen was also a refuge, a place to appear busy, with my head down, spending as long as needed being productive in a familiar way.

For me, the connection between kitchens and food stretches further than the home. I love nothing more than a meal out, sitting up at a bar, watching the chefs or bartenders busy attending to their customers and making food in an open kitchen. If I am out and I get a tall bar stool up at the counter with my kids, I am happy as can be and they know it. No stuffy table in the corner, my pet hate, but right in the centre, watching people bustling and shouting and busy. Ordering up small plates, little pieces of fish or fried vegetables, cheese and a glass of wine. There is nothing better.

I have always loved the Mediterranean. Since my children were babies, we have gone maybe three times a year. I have a wonderful memory of my daughter Zoë, aged 5, sitting at a harbourside bar in the twinkling town of Calvi in Corsica, peeling a huge langoustine with her fingers. Watching your children embrace food and become adventurous in another country is such an achievement in my opinion. I think teaching the joy that food gives is the best kind of lesson. It reminds me of a wonderful 1996 film called *Big Night*, with Stanley Tucci playing the character Secondo. Everything has gone horribly wrong, but Secondo slowly prepares an omelette and serves it to his brother and friend. Gradually everything seems to calm down and they begin to talk. I absolutely believe that cooking is the most worthwhile skill to have. You will never be short of friends, you will never be hungry, and you will never feel left out if you appreciate food and can cook.

For me, wandering around a continental market early in the morning and seeing the fish and vegetables all laid out beautifully is a truly creative experience. It fills me with excitement and awe. The displays from these loud and charismatic vendors are quite something. They create a spectacle far more impressive than anything I can think of. Pure, authentic, centuries-old and entirely captivating. Every single person who shops at the market will return to their kitchen to prepare their produce. No plastic wrappers, no preservatives, no waste, just fresh, local food prepared in a simple way. The tastes and smells coming from these places are intoxicating.

I particularly remember the early morning market in Palermo, Sicily. It seemed to go on for miles, with every kind of person from every walk of life buying, cooking or selling food. Isn't that the most basic and the most fulfilling way to spend a morning? I was on holiday with my sister and her husband at the time and we stayed in a gentleman's house for a couple of nights. It was an old and fascinating home, and his kitchen was in the centre of the house, with high ceilings and a utensil or bowl on every surface. Nothing had changed in there for decades. It was so full of soul and simple pleasures. He entertained us on his roof terrace with stories of Sicily, while overlooking the throng of Palermo, and served us sweet Sicilian wine and oily preserved olive paste on little pieces of toast. His kitchen was humble but what he prepared was a feast to us. The painted tiles on the roof, the hot sunshine and the cool dark house are things I will never forget.

A quick nip round Borough Market before a kitchen photoshoot in London.

You get a sense of a person and a place when you step into their kitchen or spy it through a doorway. I cannot resist taking a closer look, especially if the person is making food that I am not familiar with cooking. Beigel Bake on Brick Lane in East London is one of those places. I went in for a bagel and ended up asking if I could see the kitchen and how the bagels were made. Twenty-four hours a day, these cooks are kneading and shaping and boiling and

baking. I chatted to them all and we connected because they were in their safe place, and I wanted to experience it with them.

That's what kitchens do. They connect anyone who goes into them. There is no time for small talk or awkward first meetings. You instantly see their skill and hard work, the way they spend their days making a living, and you are filled with respect.

Helen cooking up some delicious crêpes for staff at Cotes Mill in our 'deVOLkswagen' food truck.

Robin has been the Managing Director at deVOL since 2011 and he has completely transformed the way our furniture is made.

Doing things yourself

Robin McLellan

My fascination with making things has undoubtedly made me look at the world differently. Once I have tried a process myself and gained some understanding of the practical challenges, I consider not just how something looks but what might have gone into making it.

I find it is the same with any craft. I decided to build a workshop in the garden and to lay all the bricks myself. I am definitely no mason, but I got the workshop built eventually and now I can't look at a wall or building without noticing the brick bond and pointing. I think design is about the detail. The way bricks were laid and the way timber was cut changed throughout history, and those details determine the character of the buildings and the period just as much as the architect's vision. If you have made furniture yourself, you see things

through the eyes of the craftsperson. You appreciate the effort that has been taken to cut a complicated joint. I used to go to local antiques auctions with my dad on a Saturday morning. It was a general sale so there was valuable early Georgian furniture mixed with much-later reproductions. I knew nothing about antiques and the furniture just had a lot number attached to it and nothing else. Considering the likely origin of a piece of furniture was a puzzle with various clues. How something was made, the wear and what timber was used helped determine when it might have been made. We didn't buy much but it was satisfying when something I had thought was good sold for big money. If something I didn't think was worth anything reached a high price, I was interested to find out why and would take another look.

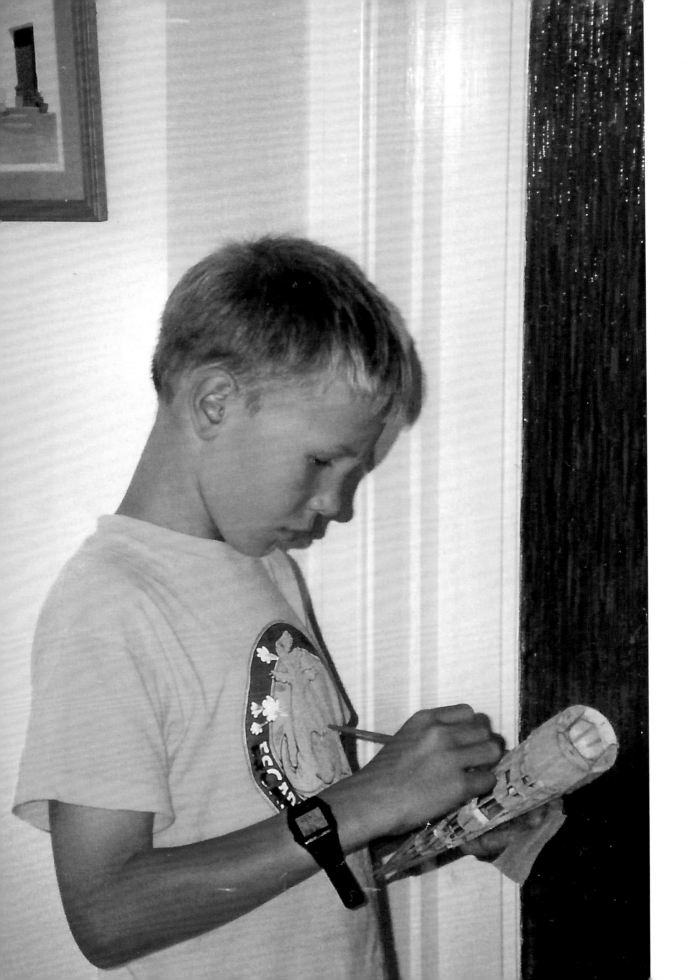

While a lot of people might not look at furniture with a view to how it was made, everyone recognises something that has been beautifully put together. In my view, good design is about collaboration, a coming together of designers and craftspeople. The most successful projects I have been involved with at deVOL have been just that. An idea often evolves from something very simple and gains momentum as people with different skill sets and outlooks contribute. It isn't that we design by committee, rather that we share a common interest and passion but have slightly differing perspectives. One idea sparks another and we trust each other's opinion.

When I was growing up, like many of us who are lucky enough, my role models were my parents, who were both teachers. My mum made clothes for herself and for me and my brother, and my dad would make us toys. If a room needed decorating, the car needed fixing or the washing machine needed repairing, there was never a question of getting someone in. They would set to and sort it themselves. Sundays were often spent at the allotment, where my parents tended to the vegetables and I dug holes in search of fragments of pottery and clay pipes. The site of the allotment had been a waste dump for Royal Worcester porcelain, so there were lots of interesting things to dig up!

Doing things yourself is fast becoming an old-fashioned notion. Doing a bit of DIY means banging together a flat pack or slapping some paint on the wall. A hundred years ago, the breadth of what people did themselves was so much greater. Things were made to be repaired and, relatively speaking, things were more expensive, so unless you were wealthy, you had to fix something rather than replace it. If you had a car or motorcycle and wanted to get to work, you needed to understand how it worked and deal with its maintenance. I like that old-fashioned notion of being an enthusiastic amateur, making and fixing things yourself and not being reliant on paying someone else.

From an early age I enjoyed taking things apart and trying to put them back together, or making things out of scrap bits of wood and metal. Lego kits never really appealed; I couldn't see the point of putting together blocks to look like the picture on the front of the box.

Wood is the material I have worked with the most. My interest in working with timber initially came from it being the most accessible material. Offcuts of timber could always be found lying about or could be liberated from skips. My dad had a few basic hand tools, most of which had been inherited from my grandfather, and I gradually accrued my own tools, nearly all of which I bought second-hand with pocket money. My passion for working with wood became more serious when I got a wood lathe for my thirteenth birthday. It was a small lathe, but it enabled me to experiment with lots of different types of timber.

The beauty of woodturning is that you can transform any nondescript piece of timber into something beautiful. I found all the different types of timber fascinating. My parents would take me and my brother on long walks in the Malvern Hills and I would pick up bits of wood from felled trees. Making something from a piece of timber I had found was so satisfying and provided my timber education. I learned which timbers were good for which projects and how to recognise the species from the bark. I didn't want to drag a piece of timber home only to find once I cut into it that it was a bit of poplar or larch, but a piece of cherry or ash was well worth the effort.

That first wood lathe lacked the power to turn anything substantial, so shortly after getting my first lathe I bought an old industrial machine. The lathe was probably 50 years old and in a sorry state, but I stripped it down, regreased all the bearings and gave it a fresh coat of paint. From that point, I was able to increase my ambitions and expand on what I could make. I built a shed in my parents' back garden to store the logs I had found. I would heat up an old saucepan filled with candle wax in the kitchen so I could dip the ends of the logs to seal them and stop them splitting as they dried out. My parents were very tolerant.

I had a free and abundant source of wood, which was fantastic. If I ever did go to a woodyard with the intention of buying some offcuts, invariably I would get given them for free. I was quite shy as a child and I remember when I went to a sawmill in Malvern, my dad dropped me off outside and I wandered in with trepidation. It was an open-sided timber-framed building and inside was a huge bandsaw powered by a very tired and battered-looking tractor. The man running the saw was operating a rack which pushed the tree trunk through the blade at an alarming speed. I thought it was fantastic: big bits of ancient-looking machinery, old tractors and piles of sawdust, what more could you ask for! I waited until he had finished sawing the plank, then explained what I was looking for. I left with several lumps of oak, which he wouldn't take any money for.

Robin designed the authentic turned oak legs of our new Heirloom Dairy Table and crafted the very first set at Cotes Mill.

Meeting people who worked with wood for a living opened my eyes to a different side of carpentry. With my growing confidence and larger wood lathe, I was able to turn objects that compared favourably to what I had seen for sale. Making things for friends and family was fine but the thought of someone paying for my work was exciting. There was the obvious financial reward, which was helpful in allowing me to further my hobby and earn a bit of pocket money. However, the thing that mattered most to me was seeing whether people would be prepared to pay for something I had made.

I picked out a few of my favourite pieces, cycled into Worcester and showed them to the owner of a craft shop. They sold paintings, ceramics and such like, and the owner seemed interested in selling my work. I naively thought that she would tell me what she would be willing to pay but instead she asked me what I wanted for the pieces I had brought. I hastily made up some prices and agreed to leave them on a sale or return basis. On looking in the shop window and seeing my work the following week, with a price three times what I had asked, I felt very proud, even more so when a few days later I got a call to say that the piece had sold and to ask if I had anything else. Selling my work anonymously in the craft shop was the first time I felt validation, knowing I had made something of value and people were impressed by it because it was good, not just because I was young. I sold work in the shop for several years and although

I would probably have made more money doing a paper round, it did teach me the fundamentals of how a business works in its simplest form. I gained an appreciation for what a nice shop could do to elevate an object, what sold well and which items gave me the best return on my time.

I was lucky enough to be part of the generation who were able to get their hands on metalworking lathes and mills at high school. While I loved working with wood, I jumped at the opportunity to work with any material and took great pleasure in learning how to use metalworking machine tools.

Our brief in the final year of high school was to make a clock. What they meant was design a clock face and stick a quartz movement in it. That didn't really appeal or provide me with much scope to make use of the workshops, so I decided to take the brief literally and make a clock mechanism from scratch. This was a bit of an undertaking and wasn't really doable in the couple of hours a week that was put aside for Design and Technology. I got on well with my teacher, partly because he was also the rugby coach and being on the rugby team seemed to carry quite a lot of weight at my school. At lunchtime he would leave me to my own devices and allow me to get on with making the clock, on the proviso that I turned everything off before I left. The clock didn't really work but I learned a lot in the process.

A view of this beautifully understated kitchen as you enter the room from the basement hallway.

When deciding what to study at university, I resisted the urge to do engineering or something that would have led to a specific industry afterwards. Instead, I chose a degree in Industrial Design at Loughborough. If I am being honest, I had no idea what career prospects it might lead to. I didn't know any professional designers or really understand how the industry worked. However, what I did know was that the Industrial Design departments had the best workshops, and I loved designing and making. I enjoyed the course, particularly the second half, where we were given freer rein to create and focus on things that interested us.

My degree course included a year in industry and that is when I first became aware of deVOL and was introduced to Paul. I had been to a few other interviews and although I had been offered jobs on a couple of occasions, I was starting to feel demoralised about what my career after university might look like. The jobs seemed to involve sitting behind computers, and if something was being made, it was being sent away somewhere else, which meant there was no opportunity to get hands-on. I decided that a job in the design industry wasn't for

me. I wanted to be hands-on, so I started the ball rolling with joining the Navy and began working my way through the interview process.

In the meantime, an email came through from my tutor about a placement at deVOL. I looked at the website and loved the fact that deVOL was a business of designer makers. The interviews were in a couple of days; it was a case of turning up and meeting Paul and, if you were lucky, being offered an interview. I had my portfolio of design work and took pictures of some of the woodwork I had done prior to university, along with a wooden canoe paddle that I had made. On meeting Paul and seeing the workshops and cabinetmakers at work, I knew I had found what I wanted to do. Paul was clear about what he wanted to achieve with deVOL. He was ambitious and had a vision that I wanted to be part of. I marvelled at the skill of their experienced carpenters like Ben Creed and lapped up any opportunity to learn more about carpentry and improve my own abilities. It felt like everything had fallen into place: I didn't have to give up on my ideal of making things and I could develop my interest in design at the same time.

Design

'Atmosphere is key, comfort is key and, of course, beauty is always the ultimate goal.'

A starting point

Helen Parker

I like to spend time looking at a room plan or sitting in the room. I seek out the features I like as a starting point – the windows, the floor and the age of the property. An older property is always easier as it already has character in its favour. Then I just look and think and imagine for the longest time. I don't rush into deciding anything. I may think back to a place I loved, a restaurant perhaps, and why I liked it. It's usually a feeling over a look.

Atmosphere is key, comfort is key and, of course, beauty is always the ultimate goal. Look at the good things about the room and build on these. Take a favourite feature, like one of the windows, and make that your starting point. Then bring in a picture or piece of art you love and prop it up on a surface.

Imagine where it might look special and keep going. Choose the spot for the table and a comfy chair and you have the beginnings of a sociable room. You need people to want to hang out in there, so give them and yourself a place to settle down. Don't look too carefully at endless images because, if you are like me, they can just become confusing, and you end up changing your mind all the time. Focus on your favourite place again – the colours, the textures and the feel – and stick with it. Always incorporate some old with the new, as it adds depth and soul to a room. A pantry is a great place to go vintage. I would always have a pantry. It is one of life's most underrated luxuries. Whether it's a room or a big old cupboard, it simply makes for a happy, contented and organised life.

Floors and windows make rooms, so make a special effort here. Plain old floorboards are always good, but if you're not lucky enough to have them, be prepared to spend a bit here. Don't spoil your room with cheap tiles. All your hard work will be undone. It's like wearing a beautiful outfit and bad shoes – it never works.

I like the sound of chatter and clatter, and the smells of cooking. I don't like clutter, but I do like plenty going on: art on the walls, crockery piled up behind glazed doors and drawers full of linens and tea towels. Try to get a few open shelves and some glazing somewhere. Variety is good, but don't do bits here and there. Commit to a long shelf and a big section of glazing. That's tough to pull off in a small room, so tread carefully here. If you have to, pick one, rather than having a little bit of both. Commitment is important. Don't lose sight of your favourite place and try to squeeze lots of other ideas in, as it will make the finished room feel confused.

Our St John's Square showroom, featuring an expanse of our handmade Emerald Green tiles with a pink wall painted by Helen and Paul, using three different colour washes for added texture and character.

Open shelving, as opposed to blocky wall cupboards, can do wonders for keeping your room feeling spacious and light.

A marble sink isn't for everyone, it will definitely mark, even after just a few uses. But given time, these imperfections will start to take on a character of their own as your sink lasts a lifetime.

I think a big sink and a big cooker make a kitchen, so, even in a small space, I would try to squeeze these in. The marble sink in my kitchen was an afterthought, but it turned out to be so important to the finished room. Allow yourself a little splurge here and there, but luxury should always be done in moderation. You don't want bling, but you do want a low-key air of quality. It sounds such a cliché, but quality really does make

a difference. If your budget doesn't allow too much splurging, don't worry. Just take your time, begin with the essentials and build on them. I would be fine with a table and chairs, a big work of art on the walls, an old cupboard for a pantry and a few really simple cupboards. Building on these bones is a great way for a kitchen to evolve, but you have to have a strong character to hold yourself back and take your time.

The starting point for this kitchen was the fabulous high ceilings which allowed the inclusion of a grand vintage chandelier.

Get rid of gadgets hogging your work surfaces. Go for pretty or classic function. A set of battered Le Creuset pans, a rail of old utensils and a well-used Bialetti Moka pot, yes! A new all-singing bread maker, no! Gadgets are a nuisance. I get a fancy coffee machine and a reliable food mixer, but all the other stuff just clogs up your cupboards.

Simple, good-quality cupboards are a must. They should be as unfussy and uniform as possible.

They shouldn't be equipped with racks and sliding gadgets. They should have shelves and that's it.

By now you should have an idea in your head, a rough layout and a feeling that you have the beginnings of a wonderfully unique kitchen. Sleep on it, think about it and jot a few ideas down. Hopefully, you have an image of your favourite place to refer to. Then, maybe look for a vintage cupboard and your journey will begin.

Simple cupboards offer the opportunity for oodles of storage and hiding away much-needed appliances.

The perfect kitchen

Paul O'Leary

Perfect for one is not always perfect for another, but over the course of 30 years, I think I have gained a sense of what most people want from their kitchen. They want something better than what they currently have, and that feeling continues with every house move, renovation and extension. As their family grows, if circumstances allow, they continue to search for that perfect kitchen in their forever home.

At the end of the nineteenth century, when people moved house, they literally took everything but the kitchen sink, because it was plumbed in, hence the well-known phrase. The rest was furniture that you could carry out and use in another house. In the 1950s and '60s, furniture for kitchens, along with other post-war products, became more utilitarian – less about beauty and more about function and economy. Cabinetmakers were thin on the ground and cupboards were made more often than not by machine. Houses were built in the same way. You can still find post-war prefab bungalows in England, built to counter the housing shortage that followed the Blitz, utilising cheap materials and low-skilled labour. The early fitted kitchens followed the same principles. Sold as clean, efficient and modern, they were a cheaper prefab alternative to traditionally made furniture. They were also modular and could be fitted into a space, from wall to wall. So kitchens were no longer something that you could take with you. They fitted that particular space and they stayed with the house.

'For me, the perfect kitchen is central to your life, and everything emanates from there.'

As homeowners came and went, the desire to improve on what suited the previous occupant became somewhat of an obsession. The kitchen has elevated in status, becoming, in many people's eyes, the most important room in the house. Understandably, the ultimate goal has become the life-enhancing perfect kitchen.

The kitchen was often the smallest room in the house, and tucked away at the back, filled with wall-to-wall featureless doors, with no room for a chair, let alone a table. We had unwittingly mass-produced the most unsociable room in the house. It took us a few decades to realise just what we'd done. By the 1980s we were knocking through to the dining room, creating breakfast kitchens and kitchen diners. By the '90s the freestanding kitchen started to make a comeback, with larger pieces of furniture that weren't fitted, pantry cupboards, butcher's blocks, dressers and the good old kitchen table was central once again.

So what's going on? Is it cyclical? Do we just like to change the way we live from generation to generation? I don't think so. I think we were governed by the circumstances following the Second World War and we were sold a line. It's not cheap and mass-produced, it's modern and efficient. We fell for it, then a couple of decades later, when those cabinets were falling apart, we realised our mistake. Now we're going back to the way it used to be and always should have been – properly made furniture in sociable spaces where families and friends come

together to share the eternal pleasures of cooking and eating. For me, the perfect kitchen is central to your life, and everything emanates from there. The perfect kitchen is also determined by the orientation of your house, by the light and the surrounding spaces. It isn't just one room. It's pretty much the whole ground floor of the house, and ideally extends into the garden and even to the views beyond.

I see opportunities to start from scratch in houses that are badly planned, with tired old kitchens. That means first of all choosing where the kitchen should be – the most important decision of all. Get that wrong, which usually means sticking with what was there before, and you may just miss the opportunity to create something close to your perfect kitchen.

The truth is, pretty much nobody has a house and garden where everything can be perfect, but it is still helpful to dream of it. Kitchen design is about how to deliver on some of those ideals by getting the best from a space. If you don't have a garden to create an outside dining area or herb garden, then you might have a balcony, or even just a window box. If you can't have it all, you can still have a little bit. Even a view of a brick wall two feet away can be brightened up by some fresh parsley growing in an old lead-lined window box. So, imagining your dream kitchen isn't a pointless fantasy. It serves a purpose. Realising a few of your dreams is immensely satisfying when you can enjoy the fruits of your imaginings every single day.

This kitchen has it all; fantastic views, a really well-made selection of bespoke and modular cupboards, effortlessly cool styling with vintage pieces and original art.

So, here it is, my perfect kitchen. It may be different from yours, and it may be most perfect for those living in a part of the world where we crave daylight and sunshine in the depths of winter.

First of all, the room should be at the back of the house, which would ideally be south facing. The sun travels across just 120 degrees of the sky in winter here, in England, and is just 16 degrees above the horizon at noon. In the summer, everything is rosy, with the sun reaching giddy heights of 65 degrees above the horizon and travelling across 240 degrees of the sky for a glorious 16 hours. This means that a south-facing back garden will get sun coming into the rooms for about 8 hours in the winter, but if it's north-facing it won't get any sun at all. Daylight and sunshine in the winter are life-enhancing and it's worth giving them a bit of thought when planning your living space. A southwest-facing back garden is supposed to be the ideal, so you can sit out after work with the sun dead ahead as you relax at the end of the day with family and friends.

I'm not done yet, so bear with me. A southeast-facing window would let in great light in the morning for a breakfast table, a south-facing window would be ideal for the kitchen sink and a southwest-facing wall would be perfect for some French doors out into the garden. Maybe it's just the English who worship the sun so much. We see so little of it that we cherish every moment. I'm sure

this is the same for Scandinavians and the northern states of the US, and in their winter the same must go for the southern hemisphere. But in the Mediterranean, southern US states and North African countries, it's quite the opposite. We might lie in the sun on a week's holiday, but the locals think we're mad as dogs, because shade is their priority.

So, perfect kitchens and indoor/outdoor living spaces are undoubtedly dependent on the climate, but the perfect English kitchen should be easier for me to define. Adding onto the back of a house does help arrange things perfectly. You can make a small room bigger and have windows facing the right way, and the addition can create a windbreak that is essential for a warm and comfortable outside meal. If you've ever lived on a hill, you'll know how wind can spoil a sunny day. In a cosy village, nestled in a valley, the day may be shorter, but without the wind, it's always comfortable when the sun shines. On a windy hill, your thoughts quickly turn to hedging or fencing, or a back addition that will create that protected patio.

It's not just climate that affects your perfect kitchen placement. You may have a lot of street noise, an unsightly view, or you may be overlooked; a back addition to your house can help with these issues too. Of course, not everyone can add a room onto the back of their house, but we're talking about the perfect kitchen, which demonstrates the ideal, from which everyone can hopefully take something!

This converted schoolhouse in Germany is a stunning example of an L-shaped kitchen. The copper worktop works so well on the island, it contrasts beautifully with the Arabescato marble and it's naturally antimicrobial too!

Sunlight and a beautiful view are good for your wellbeing, and you should try to make the best of what's available. So many people don't look beyond the current arrangement, and in my view, no amount of beautiful cupboards can make a dark and enclosed space into the sociable, uplifting kitchen most people are hoping to create. Once you look at the rooms in your house with sunlight and outlook as the priority, suddenly one particular room will emerge as the one with the most potential.

There are many other aspects to consider in that room. Size is important; a room that is at least 10 feet wide and 16 feet long should allow you to have the option of cooking and eating in the same space. In a smaller room, a wide opening into the adjacent room can also allow the person doing the cooking to socialise with the rest of the family group and visiting friends.

An island enables the cook to involve others in preparing and serving a meal. Ideally, the island should stand adjacent to the cooking area on one side and the sink area on the other, with runs of cupboards and appliances forming an L shape. If there is a possibility to include a table beyond the island with some comfortable

seating nearby, then you are lucky indeed.
From the comfortable seating area, you should
be able to enjoy views of the garden and the
cooking area.

French windows leading to the back garden
add so much to life in the kitchen. All of a
sudden, on a bright and calm day, opening the
doors and spreading out onto the patio, serving
food and giving everyone some fresh air lifts
everyone's mood. Being outside encourages you
to turn your attention away from your screens,
to notice the buds on the trees, the birds going
about their business, the sunlight shimmering on

fluttering leaves. It's at these moments in
the day that your pulse slows, your breathing
deepens and your mind ceases its relentless
random worrying.

These moments are precious, and they
brighten your spirits and encourage thoughts
of kindness and affection. In our busy lives,
bombarded by news and social chat, it's easy
to find yourself wrestling with every daily
chore. Emptying the bin, loading the dishwasher,
cleaning the worksurface in a rush with a
mind full of woes isn't the way we want to
live. It's just a symptom of modern life.

Remember when you were at school, how exciting it felt when the teacher said you were going to have the next class outside. We just don't like being cooped up. It makes lessons dull and it can make cooking and cleaning up unappealing too. It's why you should try to place your daily activities in the brightest parts of the house, where outside space is close by.

There are some hurdles along the way, of course. In an existing kitchen, the plumbing and electrics and windowsill heights are all as you need them to be. Another reception room may have low sills,

a chimney breast and numerous doors or thoroughfares, all of which complicate the placement of the cabinets, cooker and sink. That may create so many compromises that you are tempted and advised to rule out that room. But I always encourage people not to be dissuaded by their builder. They have different priorities. I would always ask for a quote to change the things that make it awkward. Removing walls, putting the plumbing in place and wiring in a new cooker point are all simple jobs, and the cost is usually a small proportion of a kitchen.

Thank you so much to Laura & Nora from 'Our Food Stories' for letting us share their fantastic kitchen photos.

People dedicate large sums to their kitchen. Some save for years, compromising on holidays and luxuries so that one day they can have their dream kitchen. All the more reason to make sure you are getting the most happiness for your money. Think beyond what's currently there and don't be put off by naysayers. Spend your money wisely to give yourself the room with the space and outlook that you crave. The cabinets, worktops and appliances are all secondary to this. Opening up a view, bringing in light and creating comfortable sociable areas will endlessly satisfy. So, take it from me, someone who makes kitchen cabinets: it's not kitchen cabinets that will make you happy. It's not islands and worksurfaces that create the perfect kitchen. It's the room, and it's how it allows you to live.

The perfect kitchen is a kitchen table with laughter. It's a quiet moment relaxing in comfort and gazing into a garden. It's a room that beckons, it's a place to settle, it's safe and comforting. It's home.

Beautifully styled Classic cupboards in Stoke Newington, London.

Classic cupboards always survive

Paul O'Leary

Our name, deVOL, dates back to 1989. My original business partner, Philip DeVries, and I needed a new name for a fledgling business which had morphed over a few short years as we tried to find a way, any way, of making ends meet. We both graduated from Loughborough University with a degree in Industrial Design and we set up a design consultancy at the beginning of a recession; work was hard to come by and the clients were tough on unsuspecting young designers. We craved being more hands-on and having a product or service to offer that was actually in demand. After a few wrong turns, we happened upon stripping doors and antique pine furniture, and for the first time, we could just about pay the bills.

Stripping furniture in a heated caustic soda tank was a messy old business. We clambered about over a steaming vat, using our body weight to sink painted pine, clad in wellies and gauntlets and rubber gas masks. Whilst our fingernails turned to brown soap and we ingested toxic fumes and lead, we were surprisingly contented just working together and working for ourselves.

We bought painted Victorian and Georgian pine cupboards from antique auctions, stripped and restored them, then offered them for sale in our back-alley Aladdin's cave. It was a time in middle England when everyone seemed to want to strip every bit of joinery in sight. Doors, floors, bannisters, windows, shutters, fireplaces, skirting and architrave. That's a lot of stripping to be done. It paid for an old Wadkin circular saw and a morticer, and a whole bunch of routers – everything we needed to make furniture.

With all that hunting around antique auctions, and all the reassembling of pine cupboards that came out of the tank flat-packed, we had somehow developed a real affinity with the detail and proportions of antique cupboards. Our first commissions were for dressers, tables and beds. Our clients wanted even more pine in their houses!

A lot of big businesses were making pine furniture at the time, but there appeared to be something wrong with it. It was orange and glossy and the proportions were all wrong, or so it seemed to us.

We had an advantage: we could make new pine look like old pine better than anyone else, using the sludge from our stripping tank. Then we realised that every time we had an original small pine cupboard or a butcher's block, a pine table or dresser base, it sold immediately. People were creating their own kitchens out of pine furniture, and any cupboard that would fit and looked the part was hot property. But there weren't that many pieces around, so we started adapting furniture and making it to order.

By that time, our name, Strippers, didn't have the right ring to it. So, unimaginatively, we combined our initials, and deVOL seemed to have more possibilities. It was over ten years later, when Philip had left to start a new life in Portugal, that one of our customers pointed out that the name spelt 'loved' backwards. Serendipity.

Fitting a Belfast sink into a dresser base, where the middle drawer used to be, created the key piece of furniture that would complete an old-fashioned, freestanding farmhouse kitchen. In our little market town in the Shires, by luck and not by judgement, we found ourselves in the right place at the right time, not to make a fortune, but to make a living, and to us, that was everything.

Traditional solid oak drawer boxes with slender dovetails on one of our new Heirloom Dairy Tables.

Right page: A freestanding Classic sink cupboard with handcrafted brass fittings, aged brass taps and a polished dark sapele worktop, in the millhouse scullery kitchen at Cotes Mill.

*Classic cupboards painted in Pantry Blue,
paired with brass fittings and a beautifully
aged bespoke copper tabletop.*

We were making freestanding kitchen furniture and for the first time we could afford to take on a handful of staff. People liked our style; it was nostalgic and it seemed to fit in with their Victorian and Georgian houses. We must have got the proportions and the detail right, because it hasn't changed for over 30 years. Our Classic English range is still one of our most popular kitchen ranges. It's not made from pine any more and it's painted, but those alterations happened slowly over decades, as tastes changed. The proportions, however, remain the same.

I used to draw furniture up by hand on a drawing board with a propelling pencil. I could have drawn the fascias thicker or thinner, introduced moulding or added interest with raised and fielded panels, but I didn't. I drew the proportions that seemed right to me. It had a lot to do with the thousands of houses I'd visited, removing doors and fitted cupboards, and the many hundreds of cabinets that we'd bought and restored. Without any determined effort, we had learned a lot. We appreciated the slender dovetails that only a time-served cabinetmaker from the 1800s could produce. We admired the slight recess under the face of a drawer knob that your fingers nestled into as you pulled a drawer open. The wide boards and tight grain of slow-grown pine, not farmed, but cut from a local copse, became something that we appreciated and wanted to replicate.

The simplicity and robustness of the construction is more akin to Irish Georgian cupboards than Victorian English or Welsh furniture, which is slightly more delicate with additional decorative details. The Irish-made furniture that could withstand many lifetimes of abuse, and it's as simple as can be. This type of furniture would have been made for common or garden houses, for traders and farmers, not for grand country estates.

It's the type of furniture my forebears would have been familiar with in my ancestral home of Kilkenny, before they fled the potato famine to make a new life in India.

If it hadn't been for the banking crisis in 2008, we might have stuck with making only our Classic range to this day. Our Classic furniture is made as a single piece; the fascia stretches across a number of cupboards and sets of drawers. So, a sink cabinet may have a sink with doors underneath and doors or drawers either side, but it's a single piece of furniture, with one fascia that is mortice and tenoned and glued together. This is the way furniture has always been made and it's very strong, providing you use timber that is broad enough. The craftsman making furniture this way has to be very experienced because every piece is different. This makes it an expensive option, and when everything's rosy, that isn't a problem. Enough people want and can afford quality. Well, they did until 2008, and then everything changed.

When people fear for their livelihoods, all projects are put on hold indefinitely. The effect on our business, on all businesses, was dramatic to say the least. Kitchen orders dried up overnight, and within a year we were in desperate trouble. I remember when there was just one order that we were reliant on, just to be able to pay our carpenters for another few weeks, and when we politely enquired just one more time whether they would go ahead and place a deposit, they told us that a one-man band down the road would make a similar kitchen for half the price, and they were going with him. We had a crisis meeting and it was clear what we needed to do to survive: learn to make furniture for half the price or go out of business. As they say, necessity is the mother of invention. And so, the Shaker range was born.

'Good design isn't just about making something as good as it can be. It's also about making something as good as it needs to be.'

We took our most popular pieces of furniture and split them up into modules. The uprights were half the width exactly, so when they were fitted side by side, they looked the same. We removed the only ornamentation that the Classic range had, a cock bead that ran above and below each door panel. We put together a range that had a few different door and drawer sizes, so that multiples could be made efficiently and cost-effectively. Adjustable shelves made standard cupboards suited for different purposes. Our cabinetmakers, who under normal circumstances may have been too proud to make furniture any other way, stayed loyal and watched as their friends lost their jobs elsewhere.

In this new range at a knockdown price, all of a sudden, those few property developers with projects to finish saw exactly what they were looking for: the right style, good quality and very affordable. The new Shaker range had saved us all, and by 2010, we were a growing business again. The Shaker sales grew and grew, and the Classic range seemed resigned to history until many years later, when freestanding furniture made a bit of a comeback and post-recession frugality was on the wane.

One of the most frequently asked questions from our customers is: What's the difference? We take that as a compliment, as it shows we must have achieved what we set out to do: make good quality more affordable. But there is a difference. We had to let go of some of the finer details that we really love. For example, to me, there are many different types of dovetail, good ones and bad ones. A good one is really slender and has wide gaps between the next. This more closely resembles an expertly hand-cut

dovetail from the past couple of centuries. But in post-war utilitarian construction, dovetails are squat, with the gaps between them as fat as the dovetail itself. Yuk! We had to accept that not everyone is a furniture geek who opens a drawer to examine the quality of the dovetails. It was the sensible course, because in hard times, people are content with good and less bothered about perfect. With my designer glasses on, with years of restoring antiques, I had been so set on achieving perfection that I had lost sight of my customers and what they see.

Lesson learned. You need more than one car in your showroom. You need to offer choice and cater for all budgets to survive in good times and bad. Good design isn't just about making something as good as it can be. It's also about making something as good as it needs to be.

Our Shaker range has proven to be so versatile over the years: understated and humble in the colour of linen with wooden worktops and painted knobs, but showstoppingly glamorous in black, with burnished bronze handles and quartz or copper worktops. It's still our bestselling range and most of the unique kitchens that adorn social media and magazines are still those very plain cupboards that are simple to make and trouble-free to use. They are infinitely adaptable, to an extent that we didn't predict. In the desperate times when we designed them, we couldn't have imagined that one day they would furnish our showrooms in London and New York, and that clients from LA to Tasmania would choose them over every other cabinet around the world. Yes, looking back, the Shaker range was a good one!

Our Shaker utility display at Cotes Mill, Pantry Blue cupboards with brass hardware.

Another great project from 'Our Food Stories'. This bright and airy Shaker kitchen is in the countryside just outside Berlin.

Urban rustic

Paul O'Leary

You can't keep a designer down. It's only a matter of time before new ideas will make such a clamour that you have to concede. We wanted to do something different. Let's face it, classic Georgian and Shaker have been done before, and although it's what everyone wants and it's a sensible investment, we're designers, we can't help ourselves!

There are other popular types of kitchen, a whole different market that sees beauty in straight lines and modern materials. Not everyone lives in old houses, and as our customers don't all come from middle England any more, we could see why they might choose something a bit more edgy.

Doing the rounds of design shows, we came across an inspired young man called Sebastian. A lover of woodland and champion of eco-diversity, Seb was

impressive. He was completely unique in his approach to design. It was all about the environment, and the product had to suit that first and foremost. The only trouble is, if you don't make what people want to buy, then you don't have a business. Not everyone is as into wood as he is, and his products were a bit, well, twiggy. Seb was drying his timber in a downstairs loo with a heater in it when we met him. He already knew he needed to think a little more commercially in order to achieve his dream of restoring coppiced woodland to the British countryside.

So a collaboration was born. In our design studio and down in our Cotes Mill workshop, over a couple of days, we learned about coppicing, split some hazel rods and tried to figure out how to make a kitchen range out of twigs.

One of the first Sebastian Cox freestanding pantries that we made is still at Cotes Mill.

We wove panels from split rods that were waney, with bark along each side. We tried to imagine how our customers would see them. Too rustic, impossible to keep clean, more suitable for a fence. So we put the cleaver away and cut the rods with a bandsaw. We took off the bark and made them straight and uniform. We wove them into panels and tried to figure out where they might fit in a piece of kitchen furniture – not the doors, not the carcase, but maybe instead of backboards they might be a bit more acceptable. We would have to promote glazed cupboards and open shelves, otherwise no one would see them. We chose English beech for the carcase, sustainable and under-used. We needed to create a market to encourage woodyards to cut it, dry it, stock it and replant. That's the goal, and it's a long-term one. Coppicing is pretty long term too. To get a strong, straight rod of any length requires a 30-year cycle. But I think everyone knows by now that the environment takes time to heal.

We liked the idea of the wall cupboards being lightweight to the eye, with maximum glass and minimum timber. Normally, the section of the timber determines how strong and resistant to bending the door will be. This is important: people don't like doors that have twisted, and if you make doors in a new way, from a little-used timber, keeping things straight will be an issue.

But we came up with an alternate theory; in a glazed door, if the timber was so skinny that it had no power to twist, the rigidity of the glass would keep the door straight. And it worked! We have the very first wall cupboard still hanging in Cotes Mill, and every time I show it to someone, I see the top and bottom catch close in perfect synchrony on the lightest of doors. Super satisfying!

Left: A Sebastian Cox prep table and wall cupboard with signature woven back at Cotes Mill.
Above: One of our skilled carpenters weaving the back of a freestanding pantry cupboard.

Light Sebastian Cox cupboards and bohemian café styling in Edinburgh, beautifully captured by Nina Plummer from 'Ellei Home'.

The Sebastian Cox kitchen display in our Manhattan showroom. This range works particularly well in contemporary or industrial spaces with exposed ducting, piping and brickwork.

> *'Inspiration comes from
> the most unlikely sources.'*

For base cabinets and upright pantry cupboards, glazed doors wouldn't do, so we designed a door that sat well with the ethos and the woven panels. It was just straight planks with a band-sawn finish. To keep the errant British beech in check, we used sliding dovetailed ash braces along the back, and to disguise the inevitable fungal staining present in a lot of British timber, we applied a dye or a colour wash. Inky blue-black and natural limed cupboards in this rough-sawn linear format were a new look, and uniquely eye-catching.

Inspiration comes from the most unlikely sources. The woven backboards weren't looking quite right. They were too uniform, too square, and just didn't look like part of a cupboard. However, I have this unique ability to watch any movie all the way to the end, no matter how bad it is. And so it was with *47 Ronin*, not Keanu's greatest moment, but set in

Japan. I found myself admiring the interiors, and there it was: lightweight interior doors that sectioned off spaces, and they were woven. They look right, I thought, but what's different? The verticals are broad and the horizontals are skinny. They look right because they have a linear feel to them, vertical lines that we are comfortable with in the back of our cupboards, because that is what we are used to seeing, with lined-up backboards. We changed the weave and all of a sudden, the Seb Cox range was complete.

The range was an instant hit, winning Kitchen Design of the Year and proving popular with creative professionals who lived in a Beverly Hills ranch or a warehouse loft apartment in East London, places where Georgian-style furniture would look completely out of character. The press around the world loved it and branded it as Urban Rustic. And so it was.

Mid-century revival

Paul O'Leary

It's kind of weird when the furniture of your parents' generation becomes collectable. My parents weren't into antiques. My dad flew in the RAF and my mum was a primary school teacher, so we moved a lot. Apart from a few craft items that reminded them of all the places that a Force's family travels to, their taste was suburban and mainstream, and to a young designer's eye it was boring and devoid of style.

But, in the passing of half a century, I guess the best of any generation becomes collectable. I spent my childhood sitting on an Ercol sofa with brown velour, watching a teak-framed telly with splayed, tapered legs, while my parents cooked dinner after a fretful day's work. We had an avocado bathroom suite and a wood-effect melamine kitchen with Formica worktops. We were all much more into gardening than interiors. But, looking back, the design of that telly and particularly the Ercol settee now have some nostalgic appeal. I even have a soft spot for avocado bathroom suites!

Over the past decade or more, mid-century furniture appeared to be making a comeback, cropping up on vintage furniture websites and eventually in some of our design-conscious customers' houses. The work of mid-century artists, like Warhol, Hockney, Henry Moore and Barbara Hepworth, has gone down in history as 'of a time', with unique appeal. You gradually become a little less cynical of your parents' generation's taste, and you start seeing the beauty in it.

There's a lot to miss about life in the '70s. Kids were free and parents didn't bother too much with them. We sat down to watch the same TV shows together as a family, at the same time as everyone else in the country. On a Saturday morning, we'd go into town to shop together, and the high street was buzzing. I used to dream of having a high street shop when I first started in business, but the high street is gone. It practically doesn't exist. In a few precious places, there still remain some relics of the past, when shopping was full of wonder. Liberty, Selfridges, Hamleys, those London landmarks are a reminder of life in the '70s. Elsewhere, the shops might not have been so grand, but every town had a high street and a few department stores. Some shops stick in the mind; in Loughborough there was a shop called Grudgings. It was, get this, a tobacconist and a sweet shop. Tins of Samson Shag rolling tobacco next to a jar of sherbet bonbons. It was a world away.

Every high street had a butcher's, a book shop, a tobacconist, a shop where you could rent a TV and, most charming of all, a haberdashery. Whether they sold gentlemen's attire or fabric and sewing materials, there was such a charm to them. They had a specific smell, as warm and sweet as golden syrup. Ah nostalgia, the privilege of age. You can remember a lot about a shop that you haven't been to for decades. You can remember the layout, the tailor, the carpet, the way the door closed behind you, but most of all the glorious array of display cabinets.

It's no wonder, with all those emotional memories, that we have a hankering to replicate something about it. The Haberdasher's range was actually spawned from a flop. But maybe if it hadn't happened that way, I wouldn't have come to the realisation that this was what we needed to do.

I took a wrong turn with a design. You can't always get it right. I thought that a retro kitchen range might be in order, something that would bridge modern solid-surface kitchens with something a bit more '30s. Inspired by Airstream caravans, vintage aircraft and the construction of aluminium canoes with a timber superstructure, I came up with a new range, the Air Kitchen. It made some waves in the press, but it was hellishly difficult to build and we only sold a handful of them. The look was half Airstream and half iPhone, and it just wasn't deVOL. It wasn't what our customers expected from us. The display lingered in our showroom for years as I struggled with letting it go. Robin and Helen told me it should go, but I was stubborn. I think all the while I was mulling over what was wrong with it and what could be changed to make it more deVOL. The curved and rivetted aluminium end panels weren't right and the flat polished white doors looked too blocky, with not enough space around them. It was cold and masculine. It was brutal.

But I thought the way the workshop had perfected making the curved frame and creating a carcase with curved metal panels was impressive. It was a carcase construction unlike any kitchen before. It had merit and it had devoured hundreds of hours

of development. I hated to waste all that effort, so I came at a design challenge from an unusual place: knowing it was wrong, not wanting to give up on it and trying to second-guess what our customers were ready for next – and it wasn't the Air range.

The rising popularity of mid-century style and the nostalgic memories of haberdashers' shops must have wormed their way into my brain, but when I sat down with Huw, our Creative Design Manager, the 3D renders didn't start that way. In fact, it looked like a dog's dinner, neither one thing nor the other. We set aside a small workshop at Cotes Mill to work on the design and Ben mocked up a single door and island base. I think you need to do both the computer-based and practical side when designing; you can change things quickly on screen, but there's nothing like seeing it full size and getting a feel for how it looks as you approach it and walk around it. When you're making experimental kitchen cabinets for the first time, you want to keep tabs on how it's looking every day. This is where Ben comes into his own; he can take an idea or a drawing and finesse it in the making. I would pop down and Ben would say, 'I've changed this. I think it looks better. What do you think?' It's such an enjoyable process.

It was on 14 February 2018 that it really started to come together; Instagram proves to be a useful design diary! That was the point when it stopped feeling like a lost cause and started to become exciting, when it felt like we may have come up with something unique that had character. Clerkenwell Design Week, where we planned to launch the range, was three months away.

We added the necessary kitchen cabinets; you need to house dishwashers and bins, or it won't make a kitchen. Flat-panel doors didn't suit the aesthetic, but we decided to take a lead from tambour-style doors that were popular in the '70s. These originally rolled up into the wall cupboard, but ours would have to be solid. We made them from around thirty oak slats slotted into a door frame, with horizontal dividers that lined up with the drawers.

The glazed countertop cupboards needed to look like display cabinets, which meant the oak frame had to be really skinny, so we stiffened it with a brass plate frame on the back. To make sure the doors opened without a fascia and without any standard fitted kitchen hinges on display, we had to make a completely bespoke hinge, so we took inspiration from another common feature in houses and factories built in the mid-century, the Crittall window. It's also having a resurgence, and its hinge allows the window to open all the way back. We made a brass hinge in the same vein that tied in with our brass frame, and when we put it all together, the design, and all its details really hung together. The cupboards made a statement, with many familiar elements that all sat somewhere between the '30s and '70s.

The Haberdasher's Kitchen sits neatly between traditional and contemporary and, for some reason, seems to be really popular with designers and creatives.

I guess, in the end, it doesn't matter where the ideas came from or how they came together. What matters is whether it works and whether anyone is going to like it. That's the beauty of design shows; they're like a premiere, and every visitor is a critic. The designers man the stand and eagerly await feedback. These days, one of the most important guides is how many people take out their phone and post it on social media. And occasionally you spot a certain type of visitor. Somehow you can tell that they've seen a lot of design shows and they know their onions. You can tell by how they look, and how they look at your furniture.

I was very happy with the feedback. Everyone used the same word, 'nostalgic', said with a smile. Four years on, I'm more than happy with the way the Haberdasher's range has been received. It's been used in the most adventurous ways, making kitchens feel uniquely stylish. It's been chosen by leaders in interior design who don't like to follow the herd, and it's been used in conjunction with our other ranges, adding individuality to a part of the room – a place for displaying cherished treasures, ceramics, linen or your favourite books.

It's a furniture range that not many could design or make, but we can do it because we have diversified into other materials. We have a growing metalware department that allows us to add strength, paring back the cabinet to reveal more of the contents, which makes a kitchen less about shutting things away and more about enjoying your favourite possessions. It just seems to make a kitchen, well, less kitcheny.

Craft

Every single cupboard is made in our workshop in Leicestershire, not something many kitchen companies can still say.

Making furniture

Robin McLellan

When it comes to manufacturing in the UK, kitchen-makers have an advantage over some other sectors. There are clear design advantages to making tailored products, and all our kitchens are bespoke to some degree to fit the space. Businesses that rely on buying in cabinets from abroad don't have that flexibility, which compromises the design, so that gives UK manufacturers an edge. However, in my experience that only takes us so far and we have always had to work hard to ensure that manufacturing in the UK doesn't come with a premium attached to it. British-made shouldn't automatically mean more expensive.

In the early days, we had a small team of experienced cabinetmakers, who would make one piece of furniture from start to finish. It was a nice way to work but it would take several years between taking

on a carpenter and them being able to make our furniture to the right standard. As we grew, we struggled to find carpenters with the skills to hit the ground running, which made growth difficult. This led to us changing our approach to furniture-making.

While it was difficult to find time-served cabinet makers, there has always been an abundance of people in Leicestershire with an interest and passion for working with wood. Some are fresh from education and looking for a career as a carpenter, while others might have served their time in an office environment and want to escape and follow their interests. We needed to find a way to harness the abundance of enthusiasm. As a self-taught furniture-maker myself, I am a great believer in hobbies and interests morphing into careers.

We dissected the way we made our existing furniture and designed new furniture, like our Shaker range, that could be broken down into multiple processes. This allowed several people to work on a single piece of furniture, so although it might still take years for a carpenter to become proficient in every area, they could become expert at a specific job much more quickly. This was a better way to learn, allowing apprentices to progress more quickly and moving away from the traditional model where the apprentice would be subservient to the more experienced craftspeople.

Starting to go down this route was not a universally popular decision, as some of the more experienced carpenters understandably wanted to continue to take ownership of a complete piece of furniture from start to finish. However, the recession of 2008 hit us hard. It quickly became clear to us all that to survive we had to be more competitive and more efficient, and everyone pulled in the same direction. The experienced carpenters helped to make jigs and set up processes to allow the less experienced ones to achieve quality and consistency, which couldn't be allowed to drop.

Making a quality piece of furniture that survives the test of time starts with selecting and sourcing the highest quality materials.

Ben Creed, our Product Development Manager, has worked at deVOL for over twenty years and is a key part of every new cupboard and furniture range that we design.

'Carpentry shouldn't be left in the past or be a slave to tradition.'

As well as looking back at the traditional techniques that we were familiar with, we had to look forward and treat furniture-making as a design problem. Furniture-making had become a bit stuck in the past. There was an established way of doing something, and there wasn't much deviation from that. As a team we had a strong design background and while we loved working in wood, collectively we had a lot of experience working with other materials. Money was tight and we had very limited equipment, so we made jigs and set up multiple handheld routers to do specific jobs.

As the business grew, we were able to invest in new technology, speeding up some of the repetitive and less-skilled aspects of furniture-making and leaving the craftspeople to concentrate on jobs that required their skills and eye for detail. Despite our reassurances, there would always be a bit of trepidation in the workshop when a new piece of machinery arrived. Would a computer-controlled router or an automated spraying machine take away jobs? The reality was, always, that they didn't.

About five years ago we bought our first five-axis CNC machine. We had some simple jobs in mind for it, undesirable and repetitive jobs such as cutting out carcase components from plywood and trimming doors. Having this equipment opened up lots of opportunities and, far from moving us away from traditional joinery, it moved us closer. With the advent of the Industrial Revolution and the leap forward in mechanisation after the First World War, certain traditional joints had almost disappeared from normal use as they had to be cut completely by hand with a saw and a chisel. By being creative with CNC machines, we were able to recreate some of these complex old joints, something that just wouldn't have been viable previously.

Over the years, we have progressively worked to finer and finer tolerances and, alongside the chisels on their benches, our carpenters have Vernier callipers to measure to the fraction of a millimetre. We find ourselves with one foot in the past and a respect for tradition, but also a desire to push forward and explore new ways to work. This approach is nothing new. Throughout history, working with timber has been at the forefront of modern technology, with buildings, ships and furniture. I feel strongly that this should continue, that carpentry shouldn't be left in the past or be a slave to tradition. Timber is one of the most sustainable materials available to us and there has to be merit in finding ways to use it as efficiently as possible and ensure that furniture-making in the UK continues to be viable and recognised worldwide.

Our team of skilled designer makers has grown hugely over the last few years and so has our range of beautiful accessories. We couldn't have done it without them!

Designer makers

Paul O'Leary

I'm continually impressed by the eagerness of new staff and their ability to pick up skills so quickly. We are fortunate to be in a place that is surrounded by great universities in Loughborough, Nottingham and Leicester. They are renowned for having some of the best design courses in the country, and the graduates come out with many of the practical skills they need to start work in a design-led company. You don't get the best graduates to come and work with you unless you have plenty to offer them. They deserve opportunities, rewarding jobs and, most of all, for their creative opinions to be heard.

A corporate hierarchy isn't conducive to good design. A good idea should be embraced wherever it comes from. In a design discussion, such as a meeting about a new range of lighting, we stand around a table with sketchbooks at the ready. We print photos of lights from days gone by and pin them up. We look at features that we find appealing,

nostalgic or familiar, and others that are incongruous or eccentric. We think about our clients and where their comfort zone lies. We sketch, tweak and assemble mock-ups. In these meetings, every opinion is listened to, and I believe the best designs are arrived at because everyone has a voice. I like to pin up where we have got to with a design, in a place where everyone can walk past a dozen times a day and look at it. You can't expect to know the best from the rest as soon as you see it, especially when it comes to the look of something. We always end up with a few favourites, and they go up on the wall. After a while, a week or two, there are some we want to pull down. They have something about them that doesn't sit well, an odd collection of parts that don't make a whole with a single character. Then there are the ones that grow on us. The more we see them, the more we see how the proportions are just right, the shape is elegant and appealing, and they do indeed have a singular unique character.

I have been a fan of the Bauhaus since I learned about their ethos at college. They did something unique. It was a time when cabinetmakers made furniture out of wood, blacksmiths shod horses and made iron gates, and tailors made suits. Everyone stayed in their lane. But the Bauhaus put them all together. Bricklayers, architects, sheet-metal workers and engineers, sewing machinists, carpenters, textile designers and upholsterers, all in the same building working on the same project. With every preconception about how something is made and what it's made from thrown out of the window, all those trades addressed the same design: the chair. A lightweight, sturdy, stacking, functional and cost-effective chair that could be made by the thousands on a production line. They broke new ground because of their ethos. They came up with the most iconic and long-lived designs of the twentieth century, all because of their ethos. Ethos counts for a lot in my book. The Czech Bauhaus Chair, by Marcel Breuer and Robert Slezák, changed our perception of how a chair should be, forever. It's no wonder that a simple tubular steel and fabric chair fetches thousands of pounds today at auction.

Developing light switches and catches at the mill with our metal designers.

In our own way, we are attempting to recreate the atmosphere that the Bauhaus pioneered in the 1930s. We have over a hundred graduates at deVOL, and they come from all manner of creative design-based courses. I love visiting the degree shows at our local universities and seeing the best graduates from across the country at the annual *New Designers* exhibition in Islington. You can see the fruits of three years of study laid out on a display board, the product standing in front of you and hopefully a sketchbook or two to leaf through. These days, with 3D rendering software producing slick graphics of every design, it's harder to see natural design flair, but it's there as plain as day in every single page of a sketchbook. Drawing is the essential skill of a designer. If you can't represent your idea on paper, to others or yourself, then you can't see the issues and you can't solve them. There's plenty of room for 3D renders and digitally printed prototypes later on, but we start with sketches and then we make models. Our tools have moved on, but the process is the same as it was when the Bauhaus were forging ahead in the world of design.

Our Metalware Production Manager, Steph, casting some of the first brass handles in the forge at Cotes Mill.

Our delicate porcelain lights were originally all wheel-thrown or slump-moulded by Kat in the Cotes Mill studio. As demand increased, we decided to start slip-casting them to her original designs.

We aren't just looking at design abilities when we visit these shows. I always have my mind on how a designer will be perceived by a customer. I might be fine with brash and cocky, but my customers won't be. I'm actually drawn to nervous applicants. I see it as a positive. Being nervous often comes hand in hand with being eager and attentive, and that goes a long way. The perfect person for a job is the person who sees it as their perfect job.

Nervousness is short-lived when the person feels capable in their job, and that's our responsibility, to make sure they are doing what interests them. It's not realistic to imagine that every design graduate will spend their whole day being creative. You can't have a business without making something at scale. But the time spent working in production gives a person the many practical skills they need to be a

better designer. Design is not just about how something looks. You need to know how to make it, or it will come unstuck. Design should run through every department, and everyone who comes up with ideas and expresses them is part of that design process. This should happen at a grinding wheel, at a carpenter's bench, even while loading a van. Every product and every process can always be better, and creative people will have ideas about how to improve things. The way it's made, the material it's made from, how it's packaged are all important, and so are the other jobs around production. Every website page, every label, every spreadsheet and every rota will always benefit from a bright spark seeing a better way of doing it. I'd encourage everyone to turn on that enquiring, problem-solving part of themselves and apply it in their work. It's the recipe for a successful and rewarding career.

Claire has produced hundreds of glaze tests over the years, each one with a slight incremental change in chemical make-up.

Our ceramics studio

Paul O'Leary

Clay, I have come to learn, is the mother of all materials. After 25 years getting to know wood and metal and all that you can do with them, ceramics became a new obsession that brought back the excited uncertainty of experimentation and took it to another level. With clay, everything that can go wrong will go wrong, and it will continue to confound you long after you think you've conquered it. But there is something very special about making things that are so shiny and permanent, things that are inherently tactile, things that become personally cherished and will be admired for many years.

It pretty much started with Claire, who now runs our ever-growing ceramics studio. She was about to do her third year at Loughborough University and was looking to work with a company to design and make a range of ceramic tableware. Our local universities know we regularly offer placements for students and creative jobs for graduates, so Loughborough pointed her in our direction. What impressed me most was Claire's hundreds of perfectly prepared glaze samples – each with a number stamped on it, which referred to a glaze recipe in her notebook. 'X' many milligrams of cobalt, 'x' many milligrams of manganese, over and over, with multiple ingredients to create the subtle differences between a deep teal, a light turquoise and everything in between. It appeared to me to be the most mystical recipe book, filled with elemental concoctions that only made sense to one person, Claire.

We sponsored Claire in her third year in the hope that she would come and work with us when she graduated, to help us set up our ceramics studio. To be honest, Cotes Mill is a pretty nice place to work, and ceramics jobs are thin on the ground, so maybe it was an easy sell, but I was still overjoyed when Claire started full time and we could get to work on some of our own products. Claire's range of tableware won some very big awards, beating all the respected and established ceramic manufacturers, so we felt like we were off to a good start.

Potters always seem to start on the wheel. There's something intoxicating about watching a skilled potter

drop a lump of wet mud onto a wheel and form it into an elegant bowl, but the making of the shape is actually the easy bit. It's what happens afterwards that confounds you. The clay dries at different rates depending on the weather and whether the kiln is on or off. If you jointed any pieces, like a handle to a mug, it may well crack. It needs fettling once it's leather hard. It can be turned on the wheel to make the shape more accurate, so that one bowl matches another. Wet sponges will soften edges and hand tools will shave spirals of clay into the air. They collect around the wheel and form clay balls that chase each other round like little racing cars. Unless you're a potter, I've probably lost you there!

Above: Jim and Jess slip-casting one of our decorative Oval Heirloom Platters in the new studio, down the road from the mill. Overleaf: A set of finished Heirloom Platters in all their glory.

Bisque firing turns the wet mud into ceramic and now it's hard, but brittle. You lose a certain number of pieces in the kiln on this firing, but not too many. It's the glazing that always seems to cause catastrophe. It's not unheard of to lose 80 per cent of the pieces you make. That's tough, days and days of work ruined in the opening of a door. There's no other opening of a door I can think of that is filled with so much trepidation. Teapots lie in pieces, platters stuck to the shelf, shards of bowls strewn around, and every intact piece is completely the wrong colour, brown instead of green, matt instead of glossy. Why? We think it cooled down too quickly, maybe there wasn't enough oxygen, it's cooler at the bottom by the door, one of the electric elements stopped working, we could try 5 degrees cooler, we could try some more quartz

in the glaze. Can you begin to imagine the life of a potter? But, and it's a big but, oh, the sweet satisfaction when a piece turns out just as you had imagined, or maybe even better.

That's the draw of ceramics. Some things are truly perfect, or imperfect in a truly perfect way. Sometimes they are completely different from what you were aiming for, but actually, much more interesting than what you had planned, a happy accident. Then the glee outweighs all the disappointments. Once in a while, a bowl that came out such a beautiful iridescent colour is sitting on your desk, days after firing, and with no warning there is a little ping and it cracks in half, rocking back and forth, laughing at you in its final moment of defiance. You have to love ceramics!

Now I see our ceramics studio growing so quickly. One kiln has become five, the first studio has been outgrown and a second opened, only to be outgrown again. We took on another big new studio, which also proved too small, just one year on. We have two or three placement students every year and a few new full-time staff a year too. Claire is a teacher and a manager now. It reminds me of our first few years in business, when everything was about learning the basics and making rudimentary jigs that would speed up one little job. We were happy that someone somewhere liked our work enough to pay for it, which kept us in a job. It's not easy to make ends meet as a potter. It's more often a hobby than a career, but we cracked it!

When I look at the designs we have created, it's interesting to see how they've evolved. There wasn't really any plan for what our ceramics range would include or what style we were aiming for. More often than not, with a new venture, you just have to get started and you make calls based on what appeals to you. It's no surprise that our designs are generally classic – we love old things and the feelings of nostalgia they invoke – but there's also a Mediterranean influence there. And sometimes a new piece of equipment leads to new possibilities.

We have so many plaster moulds, all different shapes and sizes, for casting light shades in our ceramics studio.

Hannah created our Lace Market Tiles using pieces of antique lace from her grandmother's shop in Nottingham's renowned Lace Market.

We bought an old tile press from a retiring tile-maker. It's got to be at least 80 years old, made in Stoke-on-Trent, where else? It compresses powdered clay into a solid tile. It seemed a step forward from the achingly exhausting practice of rolling out clay and cutting tiles with a metal die. This makes individual tiles all look very handmade. There's a canvas imprint, from the sheets that separate the clay from the roller, and the edges are naturally rounded off in the cutting. All things we loved. In contrast, a tile press made square-edged, very flat tiles that were lacking in character. But Hannah, another founding member of our ceramics team, was given the project of making a new range of tiles, and as it happens, back in the '70s, her grandmother used to have a lace shop in Nottingham, the home of British lace. Hannah placed lace edgings onto the semi-compressed tile and the final swing of the heavy weights left a perfect imprint, giving the tiles a unique character that instantly dated them to the various lace samples Hannah had inherited. Many of them are Victorian and impart a historic character in the swing of an arm.

We experimented with burgundy, sepia and turquoise, and the combination seemed to give off an Arabic vibe. The sepia picked out lace details and resembled henna tattoos. Hannah did the experimenting and Helen and I would each give our opinion on which colours were working and ask for tweaks here and there. Helen loved the tiles so much, they form the backdrop to her own kitchen. They have added a little Mediterranean mystique, with a bit of Moroccan riad thrown in.

'. . . this is true of all beautiful ceramics, you enjoy being close to them, they hold your gaze, and you feel the need to rub your fingers across them.'

We didn't set out to achieve that. We just made choices along the way, and each choice was influenced by the places we'd been and every sumptuous, tiled room we'd seen. That led us to create a design that conjured up a special feeling, something that would add interest and become a focal point, something that was handmade and had a story behind it. There's not a time when I've been in Helen's kitchen that I haven't noticed the tiles. They hold your gaze and as you pass by, you find yourself enjoying being close enough to make out the detail and texture of every imprint and the subtle colour variations. I think this is true of all beautiful ceramics. You enjoy being close to them and you feel the need to rub your fingers across them. Tiles, lights and tableware can all do this, but that feeling is lacking on the high street, where everything is manufactured to be faultless and anything elaborate seems somewhat fake. I think it's the connection with the maker that makes ceramics special. The little imperfections are so important; we never want to lose them.

Lighting

Robin McLellan

Lighting design is a very complex field, especially now that technology allows LEDs to be incorporated almost anywhere in your house. It's also increasingly common for them to be controlled remotely via an app to provide a very specific colour and intensity of light throughout the day.

There is clearly a lot of merit to that, and I take my hat off to the people who have developed the technology to make it possible. However, my own approach to lighting is much more basic. I like to keep things simple. While I do embrace all sorts of technology, when I am in my home, I like to interact with objects, not screens. I managed to resist having a mobile phone for longer than most, but you can't really run a business without

one, so I eventually gave in. I wouldn't be without a smartphone now. They are truly amazing bits of kit that have all sorts of benefits, however, from a personal perspective, I would say that being able to access emails and be contactable 24 hours a day is more beneficial to work than it is to family life. It is maybe for that reason that I am potentially less embracing of technology in my own home than others might be. I am aware that I look at the past with rose-tinted glasses. I am reminded of that every time I drag out one of my classic bikes and end up stranded on the side of the road or go into a hospital and see the amazing facilities. However, I think it is OK to have a romantic view of the past so long as I don't delude myself too much!

This approach is reflected in the lighting we choose for our family home. My wife and I have always bought old lights. Even when we were living in a single room together in a shared house, we would pick up old Anglepoises and interesting pieces of lighting and put them away for when we had the right space. This is an odd way of buying lighting, and certainly not a sensible one. It's far better to buy lights for the space you have rather than buying the lights first and the house later! However, the reason we did it is that lights as objects are often beautiful and interesting things and can be evocative of a time and place – from a heavily engineered machinist light that is battered and bruised and spent its life bolted to a milling machine in a factory in the 1950s, to a coloured-glass French plafonnier that might have graced the hallway of a Parisian townhouse in the 1930s.

It is probably an odd look to have 1930s deco fittings next to an industrial light and an Edwardian table lamp, but I am not a stylist. I just love interesting and nicely made objects. We buy things we love, generally for not very much money at all, and don't worry too much about where something is going until later. It does mean that we have lights in boxes under the bed and paintings leaning against the wall that haven't yet found a home, but most things find their place. I like being surrounded by interesting things that have their own story to tell, and that becomes even more special when combined with our own memory of where we bought the object or who we inherited it from. For me, that is what home is about. It is the place where we can do things for ourselves and follow our own interests, whatever they might be.

It is pretty easy to buy a single old light fitting on a shoestring, and that one fitting might be all that is needed for a smaller room. However, while a collection of different pendant lights can look good, there are occasions where I have wanted several matching fittings to give the room an authentic period feel. In those circumstances, finding suitable light fittings can be really difficult. Sets are invariably much more expensive and you pay a lot more for each fitting. Because it represents a much bigger investment, you end up looking for the fittings when you actually need them, but the thing about antiques is that when you are looking for something very specific, it can be almost impossible to find, unless money is no object.

The more everyday types of period lighting for the home can be particularly difficult to find. There are loads of mid-century industrial lights because they were almost indestructible and got squirreled away in corners of factories as people thought they might come in useful one day. On the other side of things, really grand pieces of lighting often survive, although invariably showing some battle scars. Often the more everyday lighting that might have been used in a kitchen a hundred years ago was discarded when it became redundant, as gas and paraffin lighting were superseded by electrical lighting.

When I say everyday lighting, I don't mean that in a disparaging way. We live in a throwaway society now and everyday items are often disposable. However, as with other functional items, like kitchen furniture, in the Victorian and Edwardian periods even the most basic light fittings were often made locally by skilled artisans and showed the flair and pride of that craftsperson.

We started making lighting a few years ago and in our usual way it was quite experimental at first. We made a variety of ceramic lights in our ceramics studio and while they are simple in design, there is an integrity to them, which can be difficult to find in a new product. Our ceramics workshops would probably not be unfamiliar to a Victorian potter; we have electric kilns rather than coal-fired kilns, but much of the process is the same. For this reason, our lights aren't perfect. Their shape isn't even and the glaze has inconsistencies. There is a balance to strike, as there is a difference between something being imperfect because it is handmade and just being plain imperfect. However, we work very hard to be on the right side of that line and as a result our lights have a character that is not easily found elsewhere.

Our lights aren't replicas or reproductions of period fittings. We can't replicate history and don't want to try. However, our lights are sympathetically designed and made in the same spirit as something made a hundred years ago. We value the craftsperson and the process and hopefully our lights will be long-lived enough to establish their own history.

We have added to our lighting collection recently with our Heirloom range, which has been a real privilege to be involved with. I love looking around old houses, whether they belong to our customers or the National Trust. While everyone else is taking photos of the whole room, I will be crouched down photographing a vent in the floor or a light switch. I am particularly interested in functional objects that are there to fulfil a purpose but are nonetheless beautifully designed and made. Often these objects don't catch your eye from the other end of a room, as they were never intended to be a focal point or a single statement like a grand chandelier might be in the entrance of a stately home.

Our pleated porcelain lights in New Jersey. Thanks to 'And Studio' and Nicole Franzen for sharing these photos with us.

Our plug-in porcelain beaker lights work perfectly in any room of the house. Thanks again to Nina Plummer from 'Ellei Home' for this photo of her lovely bedside beaker.

Left: This Heirloom Gaselier Light looks so grand hanging above a big Shaker island in East Sussex.

Right: The Heirloom Task Light above a sink in our Tysoe Street showroom.

I can appreciate an extravagant cut-glass chandelier or an intricately inlaid piece of furniture. I would happily own either and try to find a place for them in my home, although living in a low-ceilinged farmhouse built in the 1850s means we would have to walk around rather than under the chandelier! However, the things that interest me when I look around an old house are the objects that are below stairs, objects that have to do their jobs well and show their quality in a more subtle way, with simpler materials.

Our Heirloom range includes a gaselier, inspired by functional gas fittings that might have been used to illuminate a worktable in a Victorian kitchen or scullery, and wall-mounted task lights that project from the wall to light the centre of a worksurface. In a sense, these lights were designed to do what recessed spotlights and under-cupboard lights do in modern kitchens. I have a natural aversion to recessed spotlights, partly because I think they are boring and the light they project can be harsh, but also because I have spent too much of my time up a ladder trying to fish out blown transformers from ceiling cavities.

The Heirloom range is being expanded, as I write, to include floor and table lamps, but the family of lights will all give a nod to the brass turners and founders of the eighteenth and nineteenth century. The Midlands was the centre of the world when it came to working with metal. To our left was the Birmingham jewellery quarter and Coalbrookdale, world-renowned for cast iron, and above us is Sheffield, the heart of the cutler's industry. It feels right that in Leicestershire, in the heart of all that history, we are continuing to do our little bit to continue traditions.

Jewellery for houses

Paul O'Leary

It's always been important to fit the best-quality fittings to a fine cabinet. To my mind, having restored so many pieces of antique furniture in my early days, modern fittings are often just not up to scratch. In fact, they can be absolutely awful, ruining any cabinet they are fitted to. It has been a real quest to find the very best fittings that money can buy.

Long before we had a metal studio, I had spent several years sourcing the perfect knob and the perfect handles. Hinges had to be as they would have been in an antique cabinet. A satisfying and good-looking catch was all important, as was the feel and sound that accompanied the opening and the closing of a cabinet door. It's the Rolls-Royce analogy: it can't sound like a Citroën 2CV and claim to be better than the rest. We fitted the best that we could buy. We commissioned a wood-turning company to make knobs that were just right, from

the best hardwood, and we stained and polished them until they were very special indeed.

But although polished dark wooden knobs still suit some classic interiors, things seem to have moved on. Brass hardware became more desirable. My tastes changed too. Wooden knobs started looking a little too country kitchen and didn't match up to some of the refined properties we are now lucky enough to work on.

There were one or two British makers that were a cut above the rest, and they came at a hefty price that had to be passed on to customers. I toyed with the idea of making our own, but we weren't set up to forge handles from brass. We didn't have the right skill set. Sometimes you put two and two together and it seems like it was meant to be. Each time feels like a moment of pure luck.

My niece, Stephanie, was just completing her jewellery degree in London, so I phoned her up and said, 'Why don't you come and work at deVOL?'

'What would I do at deVOL? I'm a jewellery maker.'

'Make jewellery for houses,' I said. 'Why can't a catch be as carefully considered as a brooch? Why can't a handle be as tactile and beautiful as a bangle?'

It seemed to do the trick, because a couple of months later, Steph moved into a cottage over the road from the mill and we set up a little jewellery studio for her, probably 10 feet by 6 feet, in the corner of our Cotes Mill furniture workshop. I remember her showing us how to make a key out of silver. We had an old key that fitted a cabinet lock, and we pressed it between cuttlefish shells. We cut a little funnel shape and wired the two halves together. Then we tried melting some silver with a gas burner that we used for lighting the wood burners around the mill. It wasn't really up to the job, but it just about melted it and we trickled some molten silver into our cuttlefish shells. Without waiting, we unwired them and there was a key! It wasn't a whole key, as there was a bit missing. There wasn't enough molten silver, and it wasn't hot enough, but it was nearly a key!

I was struck by how simple it was, and all of a sudden, I saw no obstacles to making anything we wanted out of metal. We needed a big gas burner and some hefty crucibles, some brass ingots that looked excitingly like gold bars, and then we could cast something big. How exciting! So we set about designing our perfect handles and knobs. Helen would design one and I'd design another.

Mine was just a good classic cup handle, the type I would relish when I found one, but the like of which I could never find. It had to be substantial. Your fingers had to fit easily inside it, with a satisfying lip to pull against. It had to be a certain shape, not semi-circular and not too rectangular, a flattened-off semi-circle. I had it in my mind, so I drew it and Steph set about carving it out of a wax block. After a few tweaks, I was happy with the shape and Steph made up a sand box with some special red casting sand that stuck together. We excitedly dropped in a piece of ingot and turned on the burners. The solid brass that had been cut with a hacksaw minutes before became as runny as an egg and I did the honour of pouring our first sand-cast handle. I can't remember ever wanting to do something myself so much! Molten metal is somehow primeval. After breaking open the box and quenching it in a bucket, a rough-cast handle sat steaming on the end of my tongs. Steph cut away the sprue and sanded and filed it, drilled some screw holes and there it was. It was perfect.

Pouring molten brass, allowing the brass to solidify, inspecting the rough cast handles and beginning the sanding and finishing process.

It's safe to say Helen's handle was a little more imaginative, more like a handlebar moustache, but between the two, we had some unique handles that made our cabinets that little bit more special. After a month or two, we had our very own range of handles and knobs, and we swapped all the door furniture in our showrooms and updated our catalogue. Shimmering burnished brass, satin verdigris copper, sturdy blackened bronze, we had a whole range, just like that. Each of them gleamed like jewels on our elegant cabinets.

The metal studio grew so fast. We took on more graduates and bought more equipment, and we couldn't stop there. We couldn't help but design our own hinges, light switches and sockets, our own light fittings and bar foot rails. We really are making jewellery for every part of a house, and why not? Cinderella, you shall go to the ball.

Left: Our first collection of Classic and Boho handles.
Below: Polished Brass Boho Handles taking pride of place in Helen's kitchen.

Below: Classic shelf brackets and knobs, and an Ionian mixer tap all in our Aged Brass finish.

Right: Aged Brass Boho handles in a bespoke green Classic English kitchen in Notting Hill.

Functional fittings

Robin McLellan

By its very nature, furniture is interactive. Whether it is brand new or antique, every piece of furniture has a function. If I am interested in a piece of furniture, my first impression is dictated by proportion and colour, but although that is important, it certainly isn't everything. I want to open doors or drawers and get a feeling for how well the furniture is constructed, how the hinges operate, how the doors close, what the quality of the fittings is like.

The handle on a cupboard is generally the first thing you touch, and it makes a big impression. The texture, material and form all contribute to whether it feels right. For a small collector's cabinet

that won't get opened regularly, you might expect something delicate but beautifully made and accept that it is a little fiddly to use, as the cupboard's primary function is to display what is inside. However, when it comes to a piece of Victorian or Georgian kitchen furniture, you expect hardware and handles to be conveniently placed and substantial enough to use if you have greasy hands. We have the luxury of being able to incorporate smooth-running soft-close drawer runners into the furniture we make, so the effort to open a drawer is minimal, but when it comes to handle choice, if I want an authentic feel, I consider what would be appropriate if those runners weren't there.

'For me, it is really special when an object can tell its own story and provide a connection to the craftsperson.'

The thing I love about kitchen furniture from the Georgian and Victorian periods is that it was essentially industrial furniture, very purposefully built. If there was a dedicated kitchen in a house, it was most likely not the owner of the house using it. The kitchen was a place of work. This might make you think that kitchen furniture was of a lower quality than you might find elsewhere in the house, and that the hardware and fittings would be incidental. However, that was not the case. While expensive exotic timbers like mahogany were unlikely to have been used below stairs and it was more likely to be native species like pine or oak, the level of craftsmanship was often exceptional. Kitchens could be very busy places and the furniture had to withstand rigorous use with very little care being lavished on it, so if it wasn't well built, it simply wouldn't be up to the job.

This quality extended to the handles, hinges and fittings, which would have been made by a variety of craftspeople, all of whom took pride in what they did. Handles would be ergonomically placed and functional, but proportion was never ignored.

Carpenters and cabinetmakers in the Victorian period would have been surrounded by other equally talented craftspeople. There was a network of skilled traders and manufacturers in most areas. While the likes of Chippendale and Hepplewhite had their famous directories, which set out a range of furniture designs, blacksmiths, founders and tin smiths often had their own equivalent. However, there was freedom to adapt designs to suit the specific application. It wasn't a case of making do with

something that wasn't quite right. Fittings were more regularly made to measure and designs could be adapted so that stylistically and functionally each element of a piece of furniture was complementary.

While there are companies that still make high-quality furniture hardware and there is a wide variety on offer, it was always difficult to find handles and fittings that were exactly what we wanted. There was always a compromise and when you have lavished attention on the carpentry, applying a handle that is not 100 per cent right tended to take a bit of the shine off. That annoyance with having to compromise led us to start manufacturing our own furniture fittings.

We weren't looking to make fittings that made a dramatic statement, but to design well-proportioned handles that suited our furniture and enabled us to carry through our ethos in design, materials and craftsmanship. The way we construct our furniture, with a respect for tradition and an embrace of the modern, has always been important, and we wanted to carry this through to the fittings.

We had some experience of working with metal but we wanted to bring in more expertise, so we asked Steph to join our team in 2016. Coming from a jewellery design background, she had not only the experience of working in metal but also the fine attention to detail we needed. Our approach to making furniture jewellery, as we referred to it, was very experimental. We took a lead from period fittings but brought together various characteristics that we liked.

We set up a small foundry at Cotes Mill and started casting brass and bronze to make prototype handles to our designs. When you start getting hands-on with the material, you realise how important the process itself is and this becomes a big design influence. There is nothing inherently wrong with producing a drawing and sending it off to be made. However, we have always enjoyed playing about with new processes and broadening our understanding of materials and craft. That drives us to have a go ourselves. The process of making lots of mistakes and sometimes getting unexpected but pleasing results often takes us on a tangent and leads us in directions that we wouldn't have considered if we weren't hands-on.

The texture and finish on our cup handles is just as important as the form, and that is down to how they have been made. I think there is a subtle beauty in a product's appearance reflecting how it was made, from the texture of sand in a casting to the marks left by a blacksmith's hammer. For me, it is really special when an object can tell its own story and provide a connection to the craftsperson. As time has gone on, we have become increasingly ambitious with the products we have made. As designers and craftspeople, it is liberating not to be limited by one material or process. One project leads almost seamlessly onto the next, as we take what we have learned and continually move forward.

Aged Brass Scullery Brackets and Café Curtain Rails in our Cotes Mill Heirloom kitchen.

Aged Brass and Oxidised Brass Oval Toggle
Switches developed by our metal designers
at Cotes Mill.

Venturing into the world of lighting and electrical fittings, like sockets and switches, has also been an interesting journey. Designing electrical fittings, which are potentially dangerous, is sometimes anxiety inducing, and trawling through reams of British Standards and certification paperwork is not the most enjoyable of jobs. However, sometimes the greatest satisfaction is gained by achieving things that were not easy and overcoming the hurdles that might have prevented others from persevering.

What is particularly satisfying is fostering interaction and collaboration between people who have different skills, with each person bringing their own expertise in working with a specific material. Our kitchens now often combine not only the work of carpenters, but also handles made by deVOL metalworkers, blacksmith-made shelf brackets, ceramic tableware and potentially even a gaselier combining multiple disciplines.

The growth of deVOL has provided us with opportunities to follow our passions and try new things. While we always make considered decisions about which new areas we venture into, we are not held back by fear of failure. We have a wonderful freedom to follow our gut and invest in doing things we love.

These oval switches work so well in period homes on authentic walls and panelled doorways.

Style

Inspiration

Helen Parker

What inspires me is not purposeful design but accidental design, or perhaps design that is so natural it appears to be unconsidered. This, for me, is the best kind of design, so cleverly done it seems to have happened all on its own. I always feel intense pleasure and admiration for the people who display their fruits and vegetables in markets, particularly those in Mediterranean countries. I see such beauty in row upon row of stalls, piled high with produce so carefully placed and organised that it becomes a work of art. What starts as a simple metal frame becomes a stall that entices and mesmerises you. I love the fish stalls most of all – the incredible variety of fish, the colours, the shapes, the slippery skins all wet with melting ice and the frequent dousing of ice-cold water to keep the flies away.

Walking down a street in Spitalfields, in East London, is always inspiring. The variety of colours on the doors, even when side by side, always seem to blend seamlessly. The woodwork and windows are so decorative and yet so subtle, because the tones are muted or dark or muddy. Is this accidental or is it carefully considered? It appears to me to be by chance and that is the point. I strive for an aesthetic that looks uncontrived and casually thrown together, even if the reality is quite different.

Think of a local bar in Italy – pretty much any one would do – on a street corner in an off-the-beaten-track bit of town. A counter, a gentleman, some ice creams and a selection of random drinks all muddled together to make a delightfully haphazard and comforting vision. These kinds of bars excite me with their style, because it's not really a style. It's just a functional spot that has evolved over decades and doesn't change with fashion. I love the places that don't renovate and update, so you get to see things from every decade adorning the walls, on the tables and especially in the furniture and fittings.

My style and inspiration are taken from these kinds of places, places that don't do design. I love to create rooms that feel like they have evolved naturally and

Helen's inspirational snaps from a visit to the incredible Malplaquet House in East London.

not been painstakingly curated. Of course, they do take time and effort, but I always yearn to get somewhere close to the real thing. I will never stop wandering the streets in search of this, because it gives me a lovely feeling of a world where things stay the same, where they don't always have to be moving forward. Time stands still in some places, and this can be reassuring, welcoming and calming.

I try to create those emotions when I design and style a room. You know that feeling when you go back somewhere again and again, maybe your parents' house, and it is always the same, so it transports you back to your childhood? That is an incredibly strong and very real emotion. That's what a room and a place can do to you. Isn't that incredible?

What is a trend?

Helen Parker

What is behind the gradual changes in style that happen almost unnoticed over the years? In the last 15 years, we have seen a shift away from black granite to marble worktops, but now we are seeing a slow return to black granite again. We have seen kitchens in apple greens and sky blues slowly move towards soft linen colours and off-whites. Then there was a fairly rapid move towards dark cabinets, deep blues and greys, and now we are seeing a brighter and cheerier look returning, the apple greens and yellows, reminiscent of a much simpler and more classic look.

We have seen our chrome and nickel hardware and taps go from being the only choice imaginable to the less-favoured option compared to our now over-whelmingly beloved aged brass fittings. This was, in part, brought about by our collaboration with Perrin and Rowe, the dream of creating an 'old but new'-look tap that had the vintage feel without the vintage problems. All these changes in colours, materials and accessory options are natural, to be expected in the world of fashion and design. Everything has its moment, but there is a skill to deciphering what is a fad and what is a look with longevity.

*A Cornish castle by 'House of Hackney',
an unexpected mix that clashes in the
most delightful way.*

The copper accessories phase springs to mind as a fad, as it has been and gone and left its mark in many a kitchen. But even copper, overused as it was, has a place when used carefully and authentically. There is nothing more timeless than an aged copper worktop. It has a finish that is not found in any other kitchen worksurface and it creates that perfect balance between kitchen and living space, which is absolutely a look worth achieving. Nowadays, there should be a seamless connection between your kitchen, your garden and the rest of your home. Introducing patterns, fabrics, soft furnishings and vintage furniture is the key to this and has transformed the way our kitchens look.

'Nothing ever goes out
of fashion forever.'

I think you can safely choose a simple Classic or Shaker cupboard without fear of being driven by trends, and from there you need to avoid anything that feels too wow, unless it's art. You should always go for natural worksurfaces, as they don't date and even if they become less favoured, they are not unfashionable.

Remember, out of fashion can be seen as ahead of fashion! Nothing ever goes out of fashion forever. There are no hard-and-fast rules when it comes to kitchen design. I could say, 'Avoid patterned marble', but Arabescato is too beautiful to pass by. I could say, 'Avoid statement lighting', but a vintage chandelier of provenance and quality is unbeatable. I could say, 'Go light, go dark, go multi-coloured', but nothing is going to look timeless unless it has style and clever design. Some people have a knack

for picking the right things, while others have a knack for picking the wrong things. There is nothing more telling than walking into a kitchen full of carefully selected accessories and curated paint colours. It can work sublimely, or it can shout, 'So last year!' It's a matter of taste. Like dressing in the morning, it just comes naturally to some folk and not to others.

Oh, to have the recipe for getting it spot on, for being above fashion and fads and going for a look that feels already settled and at home. Trends create a contrived look. They give the impression you are a slave to fashion and you try too hard. The wow factor is not important. What is important is that your kitchen feels comfortable, interesting, calming and uncontrived. For me, this is the absolute key.

Loving colour

Helen Parker

I never think of myself as a colours person, but I definitely am. Looking around my house and in my wardrobe, it's all colourful. Not a careful matching of tones, just a huge mix-up that includes the odd stripe and the odd pattern. Strangely, I have less of a love for colour when it comes to my garden. I am an advocate of white and blue and tend to get rid of the yellow, but I'm softening up and now daffodils can rest easy if they decide to pop up here and there.

I am a sucker for pink. It's so girly, I know, but I'm ok with it. There is something exciting about having pink in your home. It feels a little frivolous and not very grown up, or at least it used to. More recently we have seen pinks become sophisticated and acceptable. Soft blush pinks and faded rose pinks mix so perfectly with sage and olive greens. The green–pink combination is one we love at deVOL. It's a mix taken from nature, which is why it works so well.

There is an air of mystery surrounding colour in interior design, a sense that there's a formula you need to know before making sweeping statements and recommendations. I think people worry more about colours than anything else. The question I get asked more than any other is which colour someone should paint their kitchen, but if I give a clear answer, it often gets a mixed response. People want your advice, but only if it suits what they were thinking. So I try to avoid the question, as I seldom get the answer right!

One approach that you can't really go wrong with would be to bring the colour in with your accessories and stick to a classic look for your walls and cupboards. Black is a good choice for cupboards, very traditional and solid. A mellow yellow is my new favourite, perfect in a dark or shady home as it really does exude warmth. But whatever colour you choose, it's a personal thing. All you need to remember is to have some cohesion between your kitchen and the adjoining rooms. You don't want your new room to have a different feel from the rest of the house. It needs to flow. Taking the floor or wall colour from room to room helps with this.

Vintage floral linens, geraniums, vines, wicker chairs and parasols, cluttering up the house and garden.

Greens and pinks work so well if done right.

Right: Classic cupboards painted in Clerkenwell Blue, paired with glossy green tiles, blush pink walls and a pistachio ceiling.

On a sunny day these huge Crittall windows almost make this kitchen feel like it's outside. Interiors and design by 'Clarence & Graves'.

There should be a common theme running through your rooms. This creates a look, your look. It becomes a trademark, so your home feels consistent, rather than like a collection of rooms that you have experimented in. A theme does not necessarily mean a specific look – say Moroccan or mid-century – but it can, and that certainly can work if done really well.

Using similar textiles, colours, tones and styles throughout your home is actually easier than you might think, mostly because people tend to have a certain taste that follows them around their home. For some reason the kitchen often used to get different treatment. It was this beacon of bright lights and sleek surfaces, but thankfully that is not the case anymore. We have learned over the last decade that kitchens are an extension of our other comfortable rooms, so we have begun to decorate them just like we decorate our living spaces, with fabrics, wallpapers, soft lamps and candles.

Classic cupboards in our St Ives fisherman's cottage, painted in Scullery Yellow.
These cupboards were recycled from a refurbished display at Cotes Mill.

From the books, to the walls, to the cushions,
to the flowers; this is a room full of colour.

I find it helps to look at your belongings when choosing colours. Maybe look at a piece of art, some crockery or a fabric that you will have in the kitchen and use it as a guide. I began with a painting and this helped me so much. I knew this artwork would be important in the room and I wanted it to fit in perfectly because I loved it. I picked tiles, wall colours and furniture colours loosely based around this painting. It stopped me having too much choice and gave me a good, limited colour palette. I like a little cohesion between walls, floors and cupboards, but more of a subtle relationship than an obvious case of matching everything. This loose connection allows for a more authentic look that won't date. I don't expect everything to coordinate, but I want it to feel easy on the eye.

This fish painting, by Wendy Prather Burwell, started the whole design for Helen's kitchen.

I find that textures are as important as paint colours. Natural products like marble and wood are easy, as they just settle in, but they are still colours and need to be considered as carefully as the walls. Try to use similar woods on floors, worktops and vintage cupboards if you can, just to keep the colour palette from getting too broad. Don't paint walls in different colours. Accent walls are bad news! I like to do the ceiling and woodwork in that colour too. I have a room full of angles and pipes, places where the room has been altered, and I didn't want these spots to stand out, so everything got the same colour, and the imperfections seemed to fade away.

Having a starting point is key, a point of reference to work from that stops you getting overwhelmed and confused by choice. Pick a painting, pick a swatch of fabric and begin to piece together your palette. Use tiles, flooring, textiles and ceramics to find colours that will not scream out but will sit comfortably with each other.

Pearl Lowe and Danny Goffey's beachy hideaway with bright Shaker cupboards and their unique vintage curiosities.

*The Sebastian Cox kitchen in our St John's Square
showroom is moody and full of personality with aged
copper worktops, cabinets and walls in the same colour.*

Buying antique furniture

Paul O'Leary

I've been buying antique furniture since the late 1980s, and the excitement still hasn't worn off. It has got easier over the years, though, as I've become more certain of what sells and what doesn't. I've become less willing to take on a project and, instead, hunt out the things that are good to go.

These days, we buy a lot of antiques. We have a huge five-storey water mill at Cotes, a couple of showrooms in London and a whole basement in our showroom in New York to fill. Every table with a broken leg or cupboard with a woodworm-infested base is a job for someone to do. If we're not careful, we find the sheds at the mill are full of things that need a bit of work. It's a business for us now, and we have learned to be efficient, buying two vanloads of antiques in a few frantic hours. But it wasn't always that way. When Phil and I started going to antique auctions over 30 years ago, we didn't know a great deal, and money was very tight. We couldn't afford to make a duff purchase.

Antique furniture was our whole business back in 1989. We visited antique auctions whenever they were on, sometimes three in a week. We'd go up to Nottingham, down to Market Harborough and to the odd one in Loughborough. They were all different, with different types of furniture for sale and different types of buyers in attendance. The smaller ones that were on once a month often had a lot of junk, and no trade buyers bothered with them.

For us, with lots of time and little money, these auctions could be frustrating. Sometimes there was literally nothing worth buying and we'd find the whole trip was wasted, but on occasion something decent would turn up and we would get it for next to nothing. That's the fascination. It's like opening a bridge or poker hand. It could be a bag of nails or the best hand you've ever seen. Even when pickings look slim, you stick around. You just look harder and imagine possibilities you wouldn't normally consider.

We always looked for the same thing, and when we found it, we could pay over the odds because we knew it would sell quickly at a profit. Pine cupboards were our staple, especially anything that would be useful in a kitchen. A dainty, glazed, pine wall cupboard with original cornice and backboards, maybe with a small pot handle and an old brass catch. If it had a lock and escutcheon, and especially the key, then it was a rare find, and we would have to compete against seasoned bidders. Everyone would have a price in mind, and a limit they wouldn't go beyond, but in the heat of the moment, maybe in frustration at

having lost some favourite lots, we would always break our limit. The alternative would be to walk away with nothing.

After a few months, auctioneers and traders know your name. They know you're not just browsing, that you're here to buy. There's a nod of respect between traders, but to most of them we were just kids. What could we know? They were particularly disgruntled when we outbid them on their favourite lot. They would shake their heads in disgust, muttering at us paying silly money for a set of Victorian bar-back kitchen chairs.

A beautiful old fruitwood table and a selection of antique kitchen chairs for sale at our Cotes Mill showroom.

Vintage chairs of all shapes and sizes will always find a place in somebody's home.

Everyone has a different shop and a different clientele, so what sells in one shop doesn't sell in another. It's an exclusive club, with only a handful of antiques shops in any county, and each one becomes known for having a good selection of something or other. The Old Bakery Antiques shop in Wymondham was great for old brass door hardware. They'd have the odd nice cupboard, if a little over-priced for us, and some decent architectural antiques out in the yard. The owner, Tina, was welcoming and always helpful, so we went there when we needed something in particular. We became known for having antique pine cupboards, tables and dressers, so by the time we had a shop of

sorts, we were regulars at the auctions, knowing exactly what we were looking for.

I learned most of what I know about antique furniture from the auctioneers. As we shuffled down the aisle, trying to keep within eye contact and close to the piece we were bidding on, they would expertly call out the lot number and describe it. 'Lot 152, the Victorian painted mule chest, nice example, original hinges, mid-nineteenth century, and it has a key to the drawer. What say you, £200?... Fifty, I'm bid.' Their expertly summarised descriptions of every single piece of furniture, many hundreds of them in a morning's auction, were a great education.

We buy all sorts of antiques, from chairs and tables to paintings, crockery and other oddities, like an old school blackboard

A nicely proportioned kitchen table is the most sought after antique piece of furniture for our kitchen customers.

These days the auction houses have slim pickings, and most trade is done at antiques fairs that travel around the country. The nearest to us is Newark, the largest antiques fair in Europe. Furniture, art, ceramics, architectural antiques like arbours and stone troughs, linens, teddy bears, telescopes... you name it, it's all there. Most sellers know the origins of their wares, so you still learn a lot about unusual artifacts. There are so many things you pick up and ask, 'What is that?' 'Oh, those are the bells that would sit at the front of a stagecoach. It's said that everyone could tell which coach it was by the sound of the bells.' Endlessly fascinating.

We buy all sorts of oddities now, not just the furniture that can make up a kitchen, but every sort of thing that you might like in your home or garden. Broadening the field of what we buy has taken me out of my comfort zone, but I'm still

learning. Helen and I always go together, and Helen has an eye for vintage decorative objects. She grew up around beautiful antiques and seems to have a sixth sense as to what is genuine. So, if it's not furniture, I always seek reassurance from Helen. Buying art is now probably my favourite thing. It's hard to put your finger on why a piece of art is perfect for someone who pops into a deVOL showroom. It's the muted colour palette, it's the fluency of the artist's brushstrokes, it's the traditional or outdated subject matter, it's the wear on the canvas or the frame, but most of all it has to have some kind of quirky character, not too perfectly painted, and maybe even unfinished. I love that people can find these things when visiting, and I love that it's becoming OK to have art in your kitchen. That says a lot. It says kitchens are for spending time in, for relaxing in and for having your favourite things around you.

Heirlooms, paintings and antiques

Helen Parker

I grew up surrounded by old things – antiques, crockery, silverware, art, maps and books. It was just the way our home was and the only time it bothered me was when friends came to stay. Then I often wished that we had cool things, new things and a more normal house. I suppose it's quite normal at that age, but I really did cringe at times.

My dad would pick me up from school on very rare occasions, in a big old car with books piled up on the dashboard. He always wore a suit and tie, even to go on holiday. Only when we actually settled into our hotel would he bring out his holiday clothes – the same clothes every single year. I can still remember each piece of clothing as clearly as if it was yesterday – the fabric, the colour and the feeling it gave me to see him finally change out of his suit. On holiday, he would still go hunting for things to take home. No lazing on the beach for us! We would visit pottery shops in Ibiza and jewellery stores in Mallorca and come home with suitcases of newspaper-wrapped Mediterranean crockery, pottery, jewels and paintings. At home, I would spend my weekends sitting in second-hand book shops, antiquarian map shops and little antique shops. I would draw or make a nuisance of myself, and my dad would chat endlessly to the shopkeepers. It was all totally normal to me.

Both Paul and I have always been fascinated by the world of vintage furniture and older interiors, as deVOL began with Paul sourcing old cupboards to make kitchens and my father was a collector. So when we first decided to display our new kitchen cupboards at Cotes Mill alongside antiques and vintage finds, it seemed very natural. It was a bit of a turning point for our style. Our photographs and displays suddenly felt more interesting and eclectic, and people began to emulate the look.

Incorporating this love of old furniture and accessories into our kitchens became ever more popular, almost expected. deVOL became synonymous with multi-layered displays that merge old and new in a way that makes a kitchen more soulful and, without doubt, more beautiful. A new deVOL was emerging, one that understood that while it takes beautiful cupboards to build a kitchen, it takes so much more than that to make it a home.

When we began buying and selling antiques, vintage furniture, art and kitchenalia at Cotes Mill, it was such a wonderful feeling. It's funny how things you barely tolerated as a child can go one of two ways. Luckily for me it was a realisation that I had been so submerged in buying antiques that I actually understood the process, enjoyed it and felt comfortable and confident in my purchases.

Paul and I make a great team and have grown to love our visits to antiques fairs. We enjoy meeting all the characters and being able to load up a whole van with exciting treasures to fill our showrooms and give our customers a little more than just a place to buy kitchens. We both have our quirks and individual tastes, which makes for a more rounded collection of purchases. We often disagree, but we often agree too, so all in all it's a fulfilling experience. It excites us and makes us animated. We are totally passionate about the whole process.

When I do kitchen photoshoots with Tim, our photographer, I often pack the car boot full of brocante from our showrooms, but I like to use items that belong to the customer if I can. Old items, heirlooms and bric-a-brac buys are always more unique than new products. They are interesting and quirky and they add a personal touch to the photoshoot that can't be recreated with new items. Often people have the most beautiful crockery, paintings and linens tucked away in a cupboard. I bring them out and can never understand why they don't display them. I find treasures that can completely transform a photograph. People love to see unusual objects in images, as it creates a story and raises questions. This is the essence of old things; they bring history and intrigue to a room.

If you are lucky enough to have old hand-me-downs that belonged to your family, you can use them to create your very own unique and personal home. Intermingling them with new items will make it feel special and different. If you're buying antiques yourself, don't feel you have to spend a fortune. It's far more about having an eye for something different. I am a bargain hunter and a bit of a barterer. I adore getting something amazing for a snip or finding something special in a tatty wet box underneath a stall. There's no better thrill for me.

The ultimate vintage piece is an old-school cupboard or French armoire, as it makes the perfect pantry. Whether you are looking for something sombre or a little more fancy, these pieces are easy to come by and can add so much character to a newly fitted kitchen. It's an easy start, the first thing I would suggest purchasing for a new kitchen. Leave it as it is if possible and maybe add a panel of crisp white cotton behind the glazing if you want to hide your everyday stuff. You can never go wrong with a pantry cupboard. It will become your best friend, something you couldn't live without.

A jumbled collection of glass cloches and pictures, pots and plants; the ever-changing vignettes at Cotes Mill.

Art can be a slightly harder purchase, especially as it's so subjective. It's the perfect antidote to sterile kitchens but it can be difficult to get right unless you have a lot of money and even then, it can go horribly wrong. I would just go for good colours in a piece that is well-executed and a bit offbeat. The important thing is that it needs to feel comfortable to gaze at. Sometimes I see a portrait that I love, but then I notice badly drawn hands or poor proportions and instantly I go off it, knowing I will never be able to overlook these annoying bits.

Everyone's tastes are different, but I would start small and go for oils on canvas – faces, flowers or fruit and vegetables. They are the most impressive and easiest to get right. Even slightly odd still-life paintings can have a real charm. I would avoid small prints in frames, unless they are exceptionally eye-catching, but I love vintage posters in frames. They will invariably be a copy, but they can still look great, bold, colourful and to the point. I like old drink ones, especially French and Italian, the bigger the better for real impact. I also like old botanical pictures, pressed flowers and plants often sold in sets. The really old ones, often European, are not too pricey. They always incorporate beautifully handwritten text, which makes them a talking point and an education too. They have bundles of charm and can easily fill a wall with little effort.

Crockery is an easy-peasy purchase. I am a little obsessed with it, mostly because it's abundant, cheap and gives instant gratification. I'm a platter lover. Any old crazed or colourful oval platter and I'm sold. I use them for every meal – salads, pasta, fruit. They make a simple meal look fabulous. There is something about oval shapes and food that works every time, and the more mixed up and varied, the better. They are so much more interesting and photogenic than a

regular set of plates. Platters are a joy to find at flea and antiques fairs and you simply can't go wrong with them. No knowledge required.

Sometimes, actually quite often, you can get a boxful of mixed crockery or a big dinner service for a song at the end of a rainy day at a fair. When this happens, I cannot wait to get home, unwrap them, pop them in the dishwasher and stack them up in my curiosity

cupboard. I have a particular penchant for majolica, the jewel-coloured plates from the Mediterranean that are often many variations of green. They are knobbly works of art and even a tomato rises to new levels when sliced and put on majolica. It can be extremely expensive, so buy a couple of really fancy colourful bits and fill in with cheaper, plainer ones. The green cabbage plates can be found easily and will give you an eye-catching, dramatic table setting.

Left page: A set of majolica plates and dishes in all the greens on a basic vintage cupboard, the perfect mix of glamour and utility.

Linens are another lovely, easy buy. Pair these with unique and colourful crockery, and you have the makings of an eclectic kitchen dresser. Take some Hungarian heavy linen tea towels, table runners and crisp French cottons, mix them with a few new gingham napkins and a big old lace tablecloth and you're on your way to Instagram heaven. I'm a sucker for a frilly, lacy old piece of cotton that I can throw on the table. Recently I've started using these linens as café curtains in my own home and in our showrooms. I can honestly say there is nothing easier and more instantly impactful than popping up a brass pole and draping a sheer or delicate piece of fabric over a window or door or behind a glazed cupboard. You are suddenly in a café in Venice, with a candle in a wine bottle, a well-ironed white tablecloth, some Thonet chairs and a rickety round table. Perfection, in my opinion, and so easy to achieve.

French vintage linens, embroidered, dyed and tied with faded velvet ribbons, with an exquisite cranberry glass water jug.

*'Be selective, be careful,
but don't pass something by
if it catches your eye. You
will never forgive yourself
if you go home without it.'*

Fabrics in general are a good buy. An old piece of embroidery or a woven cloth from Afghanistan or, better still, a rug, and you are getting into seriously good levels of vintage that can bring a whole new dimension to your room. Old rugs can be pricey, so have a good think before you purchase. Dragging a rug home only to find it's too big leaves you in a real bind. It sounds weird, but do smell all textiles before buying. You invariably can't wash them without damaging them, so if you can get a good clean item, especially a rug, you're laughing. I would only ever buy rugs from fairs, as the cost anywhere else is always too much. We have a guy we visit every time we go to our local fair. He lays all his carpets – and there are a lot – over his car so every inch of it is covered. It's a spectacle and he always parks in an out-of-the-way spot, so we can see him from a distance, this big, patterned hump waiting to be

dismantled by us so we can check out everything he has before making any decisions. These kinds of traders will give you a better price the more you buy, so go with the intention of buying a few and use them all around your home. Take your time, take measurements and commit to quantity. You can never have too many rugs.

We always go with a wish list, but we never stick to it. It doesn't really matter to us if we buy at random, because it adds character to our showrooms. However, if I was buying for myself, I would have to be a little bit more considered, because you can end up spending money on a lot of things you don't need. Be selective, be careful, but don't pass something by if it catches your eye. You will never forgive yourself if you go home without it.

Our favourite flooring

Helen Parker & Paul O'Leary

HELEN: A good floor should be like your favourite, well-worn, faithful jeans: classic in colour and fit, goes well with everything, you can dress them up or down and they are reliable, flattering, easy to look after and hard-wearing. If you are like me, then you would consider spending a decent amount of money on a good pair of jeans, because you know you will wear them every day and never grow tired of them. Let's face it, there is no better look than good jeans and a white t-shirt.

I love an analogy and I hope this one is helpful. Armed with this in the back of your mind, you can make the right flooring choice, I guarantee it. So firstly, the floor should be timeless and low-key. It should be natural, not fake, and it should blend seamlessly into the room with a reassuringly understated quality. Floors are better when they flow through your home and you don't try something different in every room. They are the canvas of your home.

My favourite floors are well-worn floorboards, wide, with a good rich colour and a smooth finish that is nice to feel underfoot. If you don't have original ones, sourcing some reclaimed ones is a good option, but a long job and no doubt costly.

If you are set on this option, I would consider you a sensible person with good taste and the commitment to buy right and fit right. If you do all this, you will be rewarded with a beautiful floor forever. It will never go out of style, will carry on ageing and requires little or no maintenance unless you want it polished. Wafting across a polished wooden floor in bare feet is sheer luxury. This kind of floor would look the part in pretty much any home I can think of, new or old. I have old floorboards in my home.

They were not in great condition and had paint, varnish and a general unappealing amount of wear and tear, so I decided to paint them all black and then wax them, to give a rich, dark, slightly reflective finish that feels comfortable, if a little noisy on the stairs! This look in a Victorian home is typical of the era, easy and cheap to create and provides instant impact. I am very happy with the look, and with a few vintage rugs thrown over the top, it is a very modest revamp.

Reclaimed floorboards of varying lengths and widths in a grand Islington townhouse.

If floorboards are a little too basic for your taste, then a parquet floor is certainly a more elegant option while still being subtle and easy to live with. In my opinion, there is nothing more chic than a beautifully polished, rich parquet floor that gleams from the sunlight pouring through floor-to-ceiling windows draped with oversized white muslin curtains billowing in the breeze. A romantic image that is actually quite easy to achieve, once you have located and bought the house with the huge windows! A dream, though, in any house, is to have immaculate parquet flooring, original or new. It is the one time when a chevron pattern is acceptable.

The existing mahogany parquet floor at
Trematon Castle set a subtly reflective
foundation for this exotic kitchen.

Flagstones are another dreamy but nigh-on impossible floor choice. Old manor houses and farms may still have some original flagstones in place – oh, the joy of finding these ancient rocks! They have a rustic, well-worn grandeur because of their size and can give a room a presence that cannot be re-created with any other flooring – pure unadulterated authenticity and that perfect old-style class that only comes from age.

A slightly more achievable option that creates a really down-to-earth, yet incredibly appealing look is terracotta tiles. These are easy to live with and work well in so many places, but you must buy reclaimed or proper handmade ones. They have got a bad rap over the years, because orange mass-produced terracotta tiles were in every country kitchen in the eighties. Cheap and instantly unappealing, they are a great lesson in how something can be so right or so wrong, simply because of its quality. Terracotta tiles are relatively cheap to buy now and have a lovely natural, earthy quality to them. They feel right and sensible and often have markings of cats' paws or leaves from their time outside baking in the Spanish sunshine. That in itself is enough to make you want to buy them! They need some care when fitting, sealing and polishing with linseed oil to give them depth and take away any orange tones, but they will reward you with a lifetime of trouble-free living. I love the simplicity, the colour, the variations and the humble look they impart—a no-brainer on every level.

A beautifully worn original flagstone floor in this Lincolnshire hall.

The best terracotta-tiled floors are full of character and texture.

Helen's kitchen has a beautiful Parisian chequer marble floor. It feels so elegant and classy but with a bit of a bohemian twist.

That's it from me on jeans and flooring, apart from to say my own kitchen floor goes against my advice above. Oh well, there are always exceptions to a rule! I went for black and white marble tiles in my kitchen. It was a gamble and a bit of an impulse decision, but I am absolutely delighted with how beautifully they work in my Victorian home.

Natural and flecked with pink and grey veining, they are my pride and joy, and I would love to follow my own advice and have them throughout my whole downstairs. I cannot speak highly enough of these classic tiles. They have enhanced the look of my kitchen beyond measure, through their unrivalled ability to be bold yet authentic.

'. . . the wrong floor can completely spoil an otherwise delightful kitchen.
But the perfect floor can easily be the very thing that makes the room.'

PAUL: For me, flooring should be classic and in keeping with the house. It should look like it's always been there. But there are many things that might persuade you otherwise. Uneven floors make fitting furniture awkward and make tables and chairs unsteady. They may present a trip hazard for children or the elderly. Large original flagstones weigh a ton and can be 4 inches thick. They're expensive and a devil to lay. If you're hoping to upgrade your insulation or underfloor heating, laying thinner, large-format tiles saves a lot of money and effort. Lining up levels between rooms is important; sloping thresholds to disguise changes in level from one room to the next are fairly obvious and clumsy looking. Laying thicker tiles or adding tiles over an existing floor inevitably means sawing

the bottom off some doors as well. There's a limit to how much you can do this. You need headroom, and the door needs its bottom rail to have its mortice joints intact, or it starts to come apart at the seams. And all of that only applies to tiled flooring laid over a concrete base on the ground floor. What about floorboards, sisal, lino, carpet, parquet, suspended floors laid on timber joists?

Flooring might not seem the most enthralling part of a kitchen remodel, but there's a lot to consider and a lot to get wrong. Getting it right is more important than you might imagine, as the wrong floor can completely spoil an otherwise delightful kitchen. But the perfect floor can easily be the very thing that makes the room. Keep it classic and consider contrast.

I know a thing or two about stone flooring through my second business, Floors of Stone. Understanding stone flooring is a bit of a geology lesson, but a simple one. In sedimentary rocks, sand and silt settle and get buried under more sand and silt until the pressure makes them increasingly hard-wearing. Fossils are visible in travertine and limestone, but by the time the stone is as deep as marble, they are gone, as the stone has experienced intense pressure and heat to the extent that it recrystallises. The appearance and texture of marble is very different from limestone, with quartz deposits throughout

and often wild veining that displays the colours of every mineral that has seeped through it over time.

Travertine has many holes in it, as little rivulets have run through the stone over millennia, causing different-coloured staining. It's denser than limestone, but not as dense as marble. The regular pitting of travertine can give a rustic and aged effect, and when grouted it looks pretty good. Property developers use it a lot. It looks the part and it's cheap, but the quality varies, and over time the cheaper materials show new holes opening up where

A brushed charcoal limestone floor runs through most of our New York showroom.

the surface was thin and has broken away. Holes can go all the way through a low-grade travertine tile. Regrouting after a year will conceal any damage, so it has its uses.

In general, limestone doesn't have holes in, so, in my opinion, it's much more suitable for a floor that looks the part and lasts a lifetime. There are many different looks; it can have a chipped or tumbled edge for a more rustic feel, but can also be honed with a minimal crisp chamfer for a clean and contemporary interior.

Marble always feels luxurious, and when tumbled it makes a beautiful kitchen floor, but a pricey one. Polished or honed, it's more suited to a kitchen surface or a bathroom, but large-format tiles with a powdery tumbled finish will transform a plain interior into something that has the opulence of a historic French château. There are dozens of other types of stone, and a few are readily available. Slate, for example, may look at home in a boot room, although darker limestones do the job equally well if you're looking to add drama and contrast with a dark floor.

'Some rooms just ooze character and atmosphere,
and it's down to lots of subtle differences . . .'

Apart from stone tiles, there is an array of manufactured materials, from terracotta to porcelain, even wood-effect porcelain laid out like planks. I think this shows just how nervous some people are about wear and tear. Personally, I like a bit of wear on a floor. What's not to love about a stone step that dips gently in the middle from the footprints of generations? But for many, cost concerns lead them to choose manufactured tiles. These do have their place, especially in contemporary interiors.

When I first started selling flooring, in around 2004, terracotta tiles were all the rage, but these and especially Mexican-made tiles, were poor quality and didn't wear well. Dog owners regretted their choice within months, and only a few terracotta floors remained intact ten years on. Spanish-made terracotta was a more even colour, with less yellow banding. The tiles were denser and more even in size and thickness, so a smarter look could be achieved with thinner grout lines.

One thing's for sure, porcelain faux tiles are getting better. In a photograph, it's difficult to tell whether it's the real McCoy or not. Even in reality, you might need to get down on one knee, touch it and even give it a knock with your knuckles to be sure. I have no doubt that they will get even better over the next few years. But as things stand, there are

some I would steer clear of and others that I would be happy to recommend. The worst for me, the ones that don't cut the mustard, are long tiles that mimic planks of wood. It's the neatness and ordered lengths, as well as the wood grain not being believable enough. It's not practical to make tiles over 3 foot long, and real wooden planks are usually 10 or 12 foot long. Therein lies the obvious difference.

Parquet tiles are a different matter. Parquet floors are made from little blocks of timber, and it's quite a skilled process, time-consuming and expensive. In marquetry-effect parquet tiles, with multiple inlaid blocks that make up a patterned square, the difference is less obvious, so there is a clear cost benefit to choosing the modern tile. Stone-effect porcelain tiles are improving every few years, and I'm sure there will come a point when I can't tell the difference, but we're not there yet, and I feel that they let a room down.

Some rooms just ooze character and atmosphere, and it's down to lots of subtle differences – a textured wall colour, a patination to the metal fittings, the brush strokes on the joinery, the original glass in the windows. The wear and character of the flooring are a very big part of this. Get it wrong and the room is spoilt. Get it right and you'll admire it every time you set foot inside.

There's no compromise on soul with a beautiful wooden floor. Imagine a Georgian manor house that has a cellar and the kitchen on the ground floor. Imagine walking in from the grand hallway and seeing faded, close-grained wide boards stretching across the room, with just the right amount of sheen to reflect the light from the large sash windows with low sills, illuminating the grain and accentuating the worn-away summer growth for that classic ridged grain look.

Here you would desperately hope to find the original floorboards, of course, but what are the chances? We've all peeled back moth-eaten carpet or scraped up lino tiles in the hope of finding something perfect underneath. Removing glue, paint or varnish can be a hefty job in itself, and most likely, not all of the original floorboards remain. When you realise that the whole floor was replaced with 4½ inch pine

boards 30 years ago, how far do you go to achieve the floor of your dreams? You could be lucky, with three-quarters of the original floor remaining, and just some rot under the windows and woodworm in the corner, maybe a few roughly jemmied boards that the plumber has desecrated when laying pipes for new radiators. That probably represents the best-case scenario, but even then, finding the right-width boards of a similar colour and patching up the ruined parts is not a given.

We have bought many hundreds of square metres of old pine flooring and often 70 per cent of it is too wormy to use. Widths vary from 4 inches up to around 15 inches. How many boards will you have to look at before you find something even close? At least you don't have to worry too much about their thickness, as it is a simple matter to plane the boards down where they meet the joists.

For new floors, nothing beats broad Douglas fir planks with a slightly bleached appearance. Some premium suppliers sell boards as long as 16.5 feet, but be prepared to spend a king's ransom. More affordable engineered wooden flooring does the job, but with pallet lengths limited to 6 or 7 feet, and boards lined up with clinical accuracy, they do not begin to fool the eye that this is an original floor.

Parquet blocks were popular in Edwardian homes and gymnasiums. They do have an appeal in the right interior, but reclaimed parquet is not an option. Originally laid in hot bitumen, the blocks are impossible to prepare for relaying, so new oak blocks, sealed and tightly fitted, are the only real option.

Getting the flooring wrong can completely spoil a room, and the main culprit is budget. I'm not saying a good floor is too expensive. I just don't think people budget for them adequately. The trouble is,

once the choice is made, you are stuck with it, and no amount of changes to wall coverings or cupboards can distract from the eyesore underfoot. With the damage done, only a rug can redeem some character.

Rugs are making a comeback in kitchens, as we all become used to the idea that kitchens are for living in. With extensions added on and rooms knocked together, kitchens can have space for dining areas and comfortable areas for lounging about.

A kitchen can be a study, a library, a garden room, playroom or lounge. There is always a business end where the cooking is done, but the rest of the space can be anything you want it to be. We love buying old Afghan rugs; the colours are bold but faded, and they bring a mystical and sumptuous feel to a cosy corner, or when laid near a fire or in a sunny spot. An Afghan rug is the hangout of choice for our much-cherished cat, who has an enviable knack for relaxation.

Laying terracotta tiles throughout the millhouse ground floor really helped make these separate rooms feel like somebody's home.

Cupboards and worktops are only part of what makes a great kitchen, it's often the final and personal touches that will persuade you and your guests to spend as many hours as possible in that space.

The finishing touches

Helen Parker

It is always fun and exciting to redo a room, especially a kitchen. It's a big expense, so it feels right to dive in and buy everything as quickly as you can, in order to get it finished bang on schedule. However, as hard as it seems to hold back, especially if you have been in upheaval for months, it really is sensible to take things slowly. The finishing touches are the part that makes a room individual and special. It is not possible to throw everything at it in one fell swoop and expect it to be right. You have to live in a space and watch the room, see how the light changes, appreciate the views, find the nicest spot to sit in and understand how you move about the room doing your daily jobs.

A carefully chosen selection of paintings, taxidermy and found curiosities can really make your home come alive.

Left: This is a beautiful setting for our Vineyard Table with a couple of candlesticks and dribbling wax, looking out over the pond at Cotes Mill. Above: Lighting plays such an important role in how your finished kitchen looks. Whether that's natural light at different times of the day or well-chosen fittings and shades.

I have a very strong personal affinity with geraniums, the way they delicately snake upwards in all directions just looks brilliant.

There is often an urge to fill every surface straight away, but a slow evolution is the key to a natural, well-functioning space. It is sensible to get some key pieces to build on – maybe a painting, maybe some large plants – and then use these to choose colours organically. I am the first person to admit to feeling that desperation to get things finished, but this is fatal, as once things are put in place it is so hard to change them, particularly if you have bought them specifically for that room. I often have the idea to hold a garage sale and sell everything I really didn't need, everything I just hung on to for nostalgic reasons and everything I bought in an impulsive hurry. But then I go around the house deciding what to sell and can't bear to part with anything. That's the problem: you buy things because you like them but then they don't quite suit, so you either leave them where they are or you move them into another room where they were never supposed to be. Sometimes this works, but mostly it doesn't, so you end up with a house full of lovely things cluttering up the places where you could do with something quite different.

I have this habit of always buying the same thing. I always buy crockery even though I have far too much, but I can't resist it! I always buy candles and candlesticks and cushions and sofas, although I don't need them. I do need coat hooks and table lamps and pendant lights, but I never get round to sourcing them. Consequently, my house is not balanced in terms of useful items. Take this as a lesson and try with all your might to hold back. Be slow and steady and careful. There is a lovely feeling when you see something and know instantly you have the perfect spot for it and can confidently buy it, put it out and use it, rather than feeling guilty because you don't need anything else and it's just another object to clutter up your home. A home is much more relaxing, calming and healing if it is functional, beautiful and well-used in every way. A small, comfy seat near the fire, a reading light and a little side table... there is nothing more relaxing. If you don't make room for these kinds of things, you should.

One-room living in our St Ives cottage; it's definitely the way to go if you find you're already pressed for space.

A stylish and, above all, comfortable sofa is often all you need to make a room feel more inviting.

Stories

There has been a water mill on this spot by the River Soar in Leicestershire for around 1000 years.

The white elephant

Paul O'Leary

Cotes Mill is a big old unit, built for work, with no ornament or fripperies. It's purposeful, slightly imposing and built to last. Our old mill is even older than you might think. It was listed in the Domesday Book in 1086 as an established water mill. The origins of this building certainly stretch back a thousand years, possibly even back to Roman times. We have found many ancient artifacts in our decade of tenure, mostly from the major Civil War battle that took place there in 1644. Several thousand troops lined up with cavalrymen and cannons in a battle for Cotes Bridge between the Royalists and the Parliamentarians. The only sturdy crossing over the River Soar was of strategic importance. Halfway between the lead garrisons of Newark and Leicester, Cotes Bridge was effectively in no-man's-land, and conquering it was the precursor to any major assault on strongholds like Newark Castle.

My first memories of this big old beast are from my year studying Art Foundation, aged 17. The mill was owned by David Hill, my photography tutor. I found him a very intimidating fellow, who often made me feel like a silly little boy. All the same, photography quickly became my passion. I loved my Praktica LTL 35mm SLR camera, bought in the summer before college. Back then, a small market town in the Shires had two camera shops that sold new and second-hand cameras. Forty pounds was a month's rent and would get you a proper camera, albeit made in the Soviet Union, but beggars can't be choosers. I loved every switch and dial of that cheap and cheerful camera. Film was pricey and we were thoughtful and cautious not to waste any. I loved popping open the black plastic film canisters and feeding the film into the camera case and onto the twin sprockets. Close the case, click and wind a couple of times and you were loaded and ready to shoot. I spent hours in the art college darkroom, slowly watching my attempts at creative photography appear as dark forms looming from the pungent, red watery trays, while David Hill uttered calm and condescending commentary. I had no idea our paths would cross some 30 years later as I tried to prise his greatest asset from his tenacious grasp.

'That humbling moment of submission is more than emotional, it is liberating. It's the moment when you realise you are OK with failure.'

In the '80s, when David Hill owned Cotes Mill, it was a bohemian out-of-town pub frequented by art college types. Thursday nights were 'Jazz Night', and for me, it was a totally new experience. It meant my life had moved on – no more boarding school, no more priests, no more parents, just people who were a little bit different, dancing wildly to the nostalgic but heady sound of jazz.

Over the next decade, like every one of my favourite pubs, it sadly declined. Every pub has its day, that perfect patch when a special group of friends and a benevolent landlord with the necessary facilities (pool table, dartboard, Guinness) come together in perfect harmony to create the most enduring of memories. I literally mourn the passing of each of my locals, and the friendships that came with them. Cotes Mill was a favourite, without actually being my local pub. It wasn't anyone's local, and as drink-driving laws and smoking bans kicked in, out-of-town pubs were doomed to failure. It so happened that I witnessed its demise slowly but surely, as it sat beside the main road to Nottingham. Everyone knew Cotes Mill; it flooded every winter, and when the waters receded, the assembled vehicles revealed the nature of the current clientele. By the '90s it was a bikers' pub in the week and a rather tepid carvery at the weekend, where grannies were treated to the most ordinary of fare. The car park became noticeably emptier as I passed on my way to work, and then all of a sudden, around 2004, the gates were chained and locked. A once-favourite pub suddenly up for sale is a sobering sight. Year after year, I passed by on a daily basis, wondering what would become of this great white elephant of a building. We were busy making furniture, but money was still tight. Then the financial crash hit the world and hit us as hard as anyone. There was a period when there wasn't a single van or lorry on the motorway, and selling a kitchen in that climate was literally impossible. One night, in the spring of 2009, I lay awake in bed imagining the speech I would give to the staff in the morning. I would stand at the top of the workshop steps, gather the twenty or so designers and carpenters around and say, 'I'm sorry. We have no work. We have no money. We can't afford to pay any of you any more. I'm afraid you will have to go home and the business will close down.'

Strangely, as I lay awake, a feeling of euphoria came over me. It had been a struggle. I'd been trying to think of ways to make a living since I left college. Now I had colleagues who had families and there was a responsibility to keep it all going. The pressure to make a sale and get a commission had become almost unbearable. But now there was nothing I could do. I could just give up. That humbling moment of submission was more than emotional. It was liberating. It was the moment when I realised I was OK with failure. The thing that I feared was upon me, but I was still there, breathing, thinking, wondering what would come next.

At the back of the mill stood a ramshackled millhouse with beautiful views over the millponds.

In a moment, I was dreaming of a simpler life without so many possessions, commitments and expectations. I felt certain I would be OK, and I slept soundly that night. In the morning, I purposefully readied myself for the last and most difficult part, letting everyone know that their lives were going to change too.

As I walked into the office, there were smiles all around. 'What's there to smile about?' I asked. 'We've sold a kitchen! It's half price, but it's work, and we can keep everyone busy and pay them for another few weeks.' 'That's great.

Amazing, well done!' They showed me the plans and we decided who would make what, while I quietly felt the promise of a newfound freedom dissolve.

When the pickings are slim, there's no choice but to become lean. We hadn't even realised how flabby we were as a business. The market had changed; there were half-built houses being finished off that still needed kitchens, but the developers would only buy from those offering the keenest price. We relearned how to make kitchens. We let go of some principles that we would have held on to before.

Cotes Mill, as it looked in 2012, with asbestos barns belying the beauty beyond.

We were old school, strong believers that cabinets should be made by highly skilled cabinetmakers who had learned their trade over many years. Before, those cabinetmakers had wanted, even insisted, that they should do everything from selecting the timber to hanging the cabinet doors. But now they would do anything to stay in work. We had to make the same furniture at half the price, or we would all be unemployed. 'From now on, Moley, you're making doors. James, you make fascias. Jimmy, you cut panels. Ben, you assemble cabinets, and Graham, you paint them.' No resistance. Everyone went about their work with renewed focus and efficiency. Just like that we were able to sell kitchens at half the price and business was easier to come by. Easier than before the crash. Instead of falling by the wayside, we were actually flourishing.

Then, in 2010, as I passed the mill for the thousandth time, the most ambitious and unlikely notion came to me. The great white elephant... Wouldn't that be something, could we possibly, is there any chance we could, imagine what an amazing showroom that would be, and a beautiful building for our staff to work in? Imagine how impressive it would look to our customers. Instead of being embarrassed by our '70s brick and asbestos unit on a nondescript industrial estate, we would be proud of our premises. The idea took hold of me, and I was giddy at the prospect. But I also knew that it was probably an impossible dream. We had around £50,000 in the bank, and the mill was for sale at £1.25 million. But I had chased impossible dreams before, and you just never know. Persistence goes a long way.

We organised a viewing and Robin, Helen and I drove up to the gates. One had been opened in expectation, and as we drew closer, the scale of the building suddenly enveloped us. There's a feeling of awe when you approach such a grand old beast. Coupled with the idea that it could be ours, it made the hairs on our arms stand up. I took a deep breath and let it out slowly. I think we all felt the same way. As we stood and admired, a distinguished elderly chap approached us. 'Hello, I'm Mr Hill. Would you like to have a look round then?'

He didn't recognise me, and I didn't recognise him. I felt admiration for him, and I felt a little pity. He quietly stooped and led us through the myriad corridors and ancient rooms, mostly unseen by all but himself. He was in his mid-70s, I would say, and he had so much pride in the building and the 12-acre grounds. I had seen this elderly chap pushing a lawn mower along the verge. I had seen him unlock the gates next to his Volvo. I had wondered who he was, and now he was right here telling his story, as the owner of this incredible place.

Since buying the mill back in 2012, it has been transformed room by room, furnished with our expanding range of kitchens and all of our interior accessories.

After he led us through the fascinating belly of the building that had been the beer cellar, we entered an unexpected space with views over the mill pond. He sat us down on plastic chairs at a Formica table and made us mugs of tea. We listened intently to the snippets of history he recounted, and we did our best to impress him. He would, after all, choose whether we could play any part in this amazing building's history. He was strait-laced, to say the least. He didn't suffer fools and was not

a man to compromise on his aims. But a little later, he led us upstairs into the mill house and we were surprised to see a makeshift bedroom, with CCTV screens all around. It turned out that the insurance company wouldn't insure the vacant building unless he stayed there overnight. The mill had been on the market for six years. This poor chap had been away from his family and unable to go on holiday all the time it was empty. And yet, he still seemed reluctant to let it go.

As I had imagined, the cellar is now an Aladdin's cave crammed with antiques from floor to ceiling, with little passageways transformed into an oasis of Helen's favourite foliage.

We added this glazed partition with
a built-in bench seat and one of our
Café Curtain Rails to create a more
intimate space.

The fact was we weren't able to buy the building with the state of our finances, and if we leased, we would be reluctant to spend the money that it clearly needed. A sensible compromise was to lease with an option to buy. I was pretty confident we would somehow find the money over the next couple of years, and I wanted to secure it and have use of it straight away. I somehow knew it would transform our business. But alas, after a few days of ruminating, he declined our offer. I had a sense that he had a bond with this building that defied rationality. After being so excited that it was nearly within our grasp, I had to swallow the disappointing reality that he was not going to be convinced. So, we walked away. The great white elephant stood there unoccupied for a further two years, and the advertised price came down and down again. Two years on, with the price at £1 million, and £100,000 now in the bank, I decided to try again. A straight purchase would surely get his blessing. Actually, not quite. He accepted but insisted on retaining the mining rights, an old-fashioned concept that dated back to feudal times. We were confounded, imagining that some hidden secrets lay beneath the adjacent field, that he needed to remain undiscovered.

We put in for a mortgage with the bank and hurriedly raised the deposit through a flash sale of discounted furniture. Anything that temporarily raised our bank balance was worth the risk – delaying tax payments, negotiating with suppliers, selling at discount to raise extra deposits. With £300,000 in the bank, we had a chance the mortgage would be agreed.

Helen and I had rented a holiday apartment on the beach in Port Grimaud, in the South of France, and we met a lovely elderly couple who owned a beautiful second-floor apartment overlooking the same beach. They'd pop down at dusk with cheese and champagne. We got to know them, and our evening soirées became a daily occurrence. Then it happened. The phone rang. It was the bank, telling us the mortgage had been approved! We could hardly believe it. There we were on the beach a thousand miles away with glee in our hearts and the excitement of a new adventure that would transform our lives forever.

After more than a decade of furnishing and dressing the mill, we know how the light changes through the day and across the seasons. Photographing rooms over and over, year after year, gives us a unique opportunity to take the very best pictures that each room has to offer.

Above: The 600-year-old stone mullions and lintel create a unique setting for one of our freestanding sink cabinets.
Right: Similarly old, individually listed wrought iron windows in the millhouse, looking over the millpond.

The grounds at Cotes Mill offer a unique experience with everything from vintage tractors to secret gardens to explore.

On our return, we just had David Hill, and his insistence on clinging on to some piece of the mill, to contend with. At these times, when you've dreamed for so long and now the deal is not quite right, you have to decide, do you concede, or do you walk away again? We wanted that mill. We wanted all of it, with no caveats. So we said no, the mining rights were a deal breaker. We would walk away. Then we waited for what we were sure would be days of deliberation followed by a resolute refusal.

I don't know why he suddenly decided enough was enough, but maybe for the first time, he did compromise on his aims. In a fit of generosity, he threw in some tractor mowers and a garage full of

equipment. The day we got the keys, it started to feel real. This was our place of business now. With a bundle of keys, we opened every door and shed, discovering relics of the mill in every corner. We rowed his plastic boat across to the island and scrambled around gauging the size of it. We stood in the grounds and looked back at this lumbering beast. It was a white elephant no more. This building had a purpose, and we were going to bring it back to life.

I don't remember ever telling David Hill that he used to teach me photography. I was sure he would remember that silly little boy and dismiss out of hand the idea that I could buy his mill.

Left: Our Vineyard Table, inspired by the traditional French version, is perfect for folding up and carrying outside to enjoy a little late afternoon sunshine.

Looking out over the River Soar on a hazy autumn morning.

Be good at what you do

Paul O'Leary

My dad never understood how I could sleep at night. 'You have no idea if you're going to earn any money from one week to the next, or whether you can even pay the rent,' he said.

'Dad! At least no one's shooting at me!' was my response.

Rear gunner Michael O'Leary, aged 19, was shot down in a Short Sunderland in the Korean War. After immigrating from Poona, India, three years earlier, it seemed like his parents' dream of a better life for him might come to naught. The stricken plane drifted for three days in the South China Sea, with its radio shot out and one of the two floats blasted off the wing. The crew lay on top of the other wing, day and night, to stop their flying boat from capsizing, and they burnt to a frazzle, contemplating their fate.

'That's what I call uncertainty,' I said, reminding him of his harum-scarum life in the RAF. Of course, when we were kids, he never told us of the countless times his life was on the line. All we knew was the excitement of Dad coming home after a few days, with his flying suit pockets bulging with chocolates. But, with us kids all grown up, I managed to prise out a precious story or two after the dinner table was cleared.

Last year, an elderly gentleman's old-fashioned voice on the phone told me, 'Your dad was the best I've ever flown with.' They had spent over a decade together flying Vulcan bombers in the Cold War. Monty had read an article in *The Times* and tracked me down to find out if I was the son of the Mike O'Leary he shared so many memories with. It was incredibly moving to hear stories from an old friend, five years after my dad's passing. And it reminded me of the one and only piece of advice my dad ever gave me: 'Be good at what you do.'

I was always going to be 'in business'. I'd tried working for other people and it didn't go well for me. My first job, at 50p per hour, was working in the fields budding rose stems. Actually, someone skilled did that; I just followed behind in a permanent stoop wrapping rubber bands around the graft. Fifty pence an hour was riches, but every morning when I was picked up on the main road, I had to endure the ritual welcome from the lads in the truck, enquiring whether parts of my anatomy may have matured since yesterday.

When I was at college, you either signed on for the dole in the holidays or you worked as a temp. I didn't like the Job Centre, and it didn't feel right. I wasn't really unemployed. I was a student, one of the layabouts, as we were collectively referred to. So I did bar work, waitering at events, working in a print room basement, and shifts at Walkers Crisps in the holidays.

Walkers had a 'How could this happen?' board. There were packets with the writing halfway up, and packets with black crisps in, and one particularly notorious packet that had a single, washed, whole, but uncooked potato in it. How could this happen indeed!

I worked on the wet line, where the potatoes were washed. Workers lined the conveyor chopping the big ones in half and flinging the black ones over the opposite line of people into skips for pig feed.

The jobs were routine, but the pace of my co-workers was astounding. I'd think through every move, watch and study techniques, practise and adjust to try to catch up, but I was never as fast as them. Eventually, though, even in such a noisy, manic place, I managed to find a calmness that allowed my mind to wander. I imagined impressing a supervisor with my great ideas and being asked to work in the office.

After a few more days of chopping and flinging, I spent some hours at home preparing a report: 'Saving wastage on the wet line.' Catchy! Within my neatly titled and bound file were graphs on potato prices, man hours to chop out black bits, saved transport costs, estimated savings for varying degrees of rot. I was sure that was my ticket off the wet line.

So I called in to the production manager's office and hung around until the end of my break, but with no sign of him, I left the report on his desk with a Post-it saying, 'Please read me.' Then I went back to the wet line, chopping and flinging. Would he read it today and come and find me? Probably not until tomorrow. That's more realistic. He's a busy guy. Maybe he'll want to show it to his boss. Maybe he needs to check my figures, so he can tell me what I got right and what was wrong. Definitely by the end of the week, he'll come down the line and ask the supervisor, who'll point in my direction, and he'll walk over smiling and shake my hand.

He didn't come. I waited weeks. Hopes were dashed and resentment kicked in. I was done with Walkers. I was done with working! I can't say I blame anyone. Did I have any business thinking they could learn anything from me?

So, from around the end of my second year studying product design at Loughborough University, I decided I would make my own way in life. No job interviews, no hierarchy, no rejection. I'd think of jobs that would be fun and do them with my mates. And so followed the litany of heroic failures.

Top: The back garden of our RAF quarters in Cyprus in the late 1960s.

Below: The O'Leary family at the RAF beach in Cyprus.

A slightly unconventional life

Helen Parker

As a child, I was not academic. I was a little wayward, I think! I was the girl who created mischief and did not concentrate or work hard. I lived a slightly unconventional life, I guess. Everyone's life is different, and everyone has a story to tell, so I don't suppose I can blame anyone or anything.

My father was an academic. He was full of character and intrigue and our home was filled with books, pottery, maps, antiques and memories of his life. My mother left when I was two and my eldest sister was 10. I don't remember her and didn't see her again until I was 15. My grandmother came to live with us when we were young and then my father remarried, and I had another sister 10 years younger than me. My eldest sister went away to

boarding school, so I was a bit of a loner. I still am. We lived in a large Victorian house in a village in Nottinghamshire. I liked it there because I had lots of freedom. I had space and could escape to my own world and explore. I spent endless days looking for secrets, opening my father's wardrobes and finding boxes with photographs of my mother. I lost myself in my grandma's wardrobes, filled with jewellery and handbags, dresses, furs and long calfskin gloves soft as butter. It seemed never-ending. Outside, there were stables, garages and outhouses full of tea chests crammed with newspaper-wrapped pottery and china, or old cars piled high with books and maps. I was surrounded by old things, memories I tried to make sense of and things that fascinated and puzzled me.

Helen's father (centre), Arthur Rodgers.

I lived at the top of the house. I had a whole floor to myself – a bathroom, a bedroom, a storeroom (full of magazines, books and letters) and a big open living space, which was filled with furniture and beds, chests of drawers and paintings. Even though it was full of old things, I made it my own. It was a little like living in a very large shop. But I changed it about all the time and I liked it because I could do what I wanted. I bought some wallpaper from a jumble sale and re-decorated my bathroom. I loved my bathroom; it had a lock on the door, and I could climb out of the window onto the roof and watch the world go by, or have a secret smoke when I got older.

I never considered until much later in life that this house and all its things made me resourceful. It captured a part of me that was not apparent to my father or my teachers. I believe it brought out the designer in me, the person who loves nothing more than to work with what I have and create something. It's hard to see the connection when you are young, the link between what you find intriguing and creative and what you may want to do with your life when you are older. I am sure if my children had done these things, I would have seen a talent and steered them in that direction, but for me it went unnoticed. My father probably despaired of me because I was simply not motivated by school at all. I loved to make things, design things and draw but I couldn't understand the concepts of maths or science. They went right over my head. Making things, changing things and trying to get the best out of what I had was what made me tick.

My father was different from other fathers. He taught me the names of flowers, trees and birds. He took me to bookshops, markets and antique shops. He taught me the importance of writing a good letter and he read to me. He didn't fuss over us, but he loved us. At Christmas, he would go into his cupboards, cars and outhouses to find us presents – a book or a picture or an old piece of jewellery. He didn't go Christmas shopping. He bought things when he saw them, kept them and then tried to find them when needed. If I needed clothes, he would call up his friend who had a warehouse in a dodgy part of Nottingham, and he would take me in the evening. They would switch the lights on in the warehouse and leave me to it while they chatted and drank tea. An hour or so later, I would come out with piles of clothes in cellophane wrappers and my father would barter a price. He was a raconteur and a true gentleman, but he loved a bargain. Back home, I would unwrap the stash and hope for the best. Maybe a few alterations were needed. Tony was another of my father's market mates. He sold old broken jewellery in clear plastic bags for 50p. These were the best fun – getting home, tipping out the glistening tangle of chains and jewels and deciding how best to make them wearable. I went on to create a little collection of earrings that were quite desirable. Liberty in London bought them off me and sold them in their store. Still, I didn't get the calling to become a designer or follow it as a career. It was just a nice little story, and I never did it again.

Time was running out for me. I was sixteen by now and I had three O Levels – Art, Cookery and English, all grade A – but nothing else. I find it quite strange that to this day, they are the things I am good at. I didn't have the necessary requirements to do A Levels, so my father called up some friends and managed to get me onto a secretarial course at a college in Nottingham. Looking back, it was madness. I never could have made it as a secretary, and I had no intention of even trying. It did lead me to do an evening class to gain an A Level in Art, so all was not lost. I loved the night class, and, in the life modelling classes, I sometimes stepped in as the model and made a few pounds to boot. But after getting thrown off the secretarial course and gaining an A in A Level Art, I still didn't see the calling.

I went on to do another course, in Beauty Therapy. I enjoyed it, and I moved to Sheffield, where I got a job working in a salon. I did OK but it wasn't really me. Wearing a white overall and all that neat and tidy stuff didn't feel right. I moved back home for a while and started working in a clothes shop.

Fast forward to having my children and being a married woman. Life was good. I was back in the home, back in the kitchen and finally feeling like I belonged again. I just wasn't cut out for having a job. They were a means to an end and I actually feel quite embarrassed now to remember my lack of motivation to make something of myself. But I did make something of myself. I made myself a mother and it was the most important and fulfilling job I had ever dreamed of. I often think that my lack of ambition workwise was a sort of backhanded

blessing, because it allowed me to dedicate myself to my children and my home without the struggle and dilemma that people have when juggling careers and children.

I found a notebook the other day when my son Max was home visiting. It was a guide I'd written for my sister to follow when I went into the hospital to have my daughter Zoë. It listed the things Max liked to eat, which included crusty French bread and butter and spaghetti with fresh parmesan. He was only two! We laughed together and I knew he would understand how important this was to me. My children, their friends and families, my friends and family and my home all gave me the chance to love, to cook, to be creative, make a home and feel I had found my place in this world, finally.

Left: Helen looking pretty rock and roll, back in the '80s.
Above: Helen, styling in the Haberdasher's Kitchen at Cotes Mill, Leicestershire.

The job of my dreams

Helen Parker

Time moves on and my children were growing up fast. Their lives were full and they no longer needed to be looked after and entertained at home. They had sports to play and parties to go to and friends to spend their time with. I enjoyed the new chapter and the changing role I played in their lives, but I had to fill my days with something other than home, so I got a job at their school, looking after children who needed a little more help during their school day. It was nice to earn a little money and have a new purpose, but still it didn't excite me. The children moved school and I left too and thought about what else I could do.

I saw an advert in the local newspaper. A small deli in a village outside my hometown was looking for help. Brewing coffee and making sandwiches, slicing ham and putting pies in paper bags – it was just right for me. I took to the role naturally and happily, and even though my home life was in turmoil, I was content at work. The village was busy, and all sorts of folk popped in for a lunchtime snack. Being in a kitchen once again made me feel comfortable and at ease.

Leaving the deli one afternoon, I dashed across the road and got in my car to head home when a man jumped into my passenger seat. It was a guy I had a vague memory of from my younger days. He owned a small kitchen shop in the village, a pretty little old-fashioned shop. In the window, there were always beautiful cupboards with Belfast sinks in them and butcher's blocks painted in soft, muted colours. I always admired the window as I drove past. It was unusual in its simplicity and style and it stood out as being different and carefully considered. If it had been today, I would have taken a photograph on my phone and popped it on my Instagram with the hashtag 'totallydreamyenglishkitchens'.

Anyway, back to the slightly odd moment when this man had invited himself into my passenger seat. He asked me if I enjoyed my job at the deli. 'Yes, thanks, I do,' I said, with a confused smile. 'How do you fancy designing kitchens?' he asked. 'Oh, I couldn't possibly do that,' I said, hoping he would get out quickly and never find out I could barely use a computer and had no qualifications. He proceeded to say that he thought I would be perfect to chat to his customers, as I was relatable and friendly. I embarrassedly thanked him for his complimentary words and his time and said unfortunately it wouldn't be something I could do. He persisted and asked if I could draw, to which I happily replied, 'Yes.' 'Well, would you go home and draw up your kitchen and write me a letter describing how you might like to change it?' he asked. I hesitantly agreed. Goodness only knows why, but on reflection, it was not a bad time to say yes!

He then chatted about his kitchen business, deVOL, in such a passionate and excitable way. He was full of energy and enthusiasm, and I was completely panic-stricken, but bowled over by this meeting. He was about my age, but looked much younger. He was handsome, very handsome, and had an unpretentious confidence that I really liked. His name was Paul O'Leary.

The next 24 hours were a blind panic. I obviously couldn't be a kitchen designer, but I didn't want to let myself down and I did want to impress Paul. The ideal scenario would be if I sent what he'd asked for and he replied saying, 'Your letter and drawings are beautifully presented, very well executed and written, but unfortunately we don't now have a vacancy.'

With graph paper, Rotring pens and my treasured ink pen, I set to work. I measured up my kitchen and made a start on the way I wanted my project to look. It was a long job. I was absolutely determined to pretend I had some skills. I am not sure I had ever concentrated so hard on anything for such a long time, but finally, I was completely happy with the contents of the crisp white A4 envelope, the address

on the front handwritten in blue-black ink. It all felt slightly surreal, sort of futile really, because I was never going to get a job as a kitchen designer in a beautiful little showroom with a man who clearly had something special going on. A day or so later I had a call. 'Hi Helen, it's Paul here. Thanks so much for your letter. Would you be available to have a chat with me and my manager Lesley?' I thought, what a fine mess I've got myself into, but I said, 'Yes, of course. That would be great.'

Paul and Lesley visited me at home. Lesley was lovely and we chatted away, although I can't remember a word of our conversation. They left cheerfully and said they would be in touch. I realised I had probably just had an interview. I closed the door and thought, phew! A minute later, the doorbell rang, and it was Paul again. 'We think you would be perfect,' he said. 'Lesley and I would love you to come in for a few days and see how you get on.'

So many thoughts ran through my head. What will I wear? What will I say about computers? How will I cope? What if they suddenly realise I am a fraud and it's all awfully embarrassing for everyone when they ask me to leave? They didn't ask me to leave. They still haven't. It's been nearly 18 years. I wonder if I've pulled it off!

Did I really get a job designing kitchens in a beautiful showroom with a handful of the most delightful people to help and support me? Did I get complimented and congratulated by Paul for doing a great job and offered his expert help whenever I needed it? I think I did. I think I managed to pull off the biggest scam of my life. Or maybe, just maybe, my life up to that point had all been preparation for that moment. The three O Levels in Art, English and Cookery, the importance of writing a good letter and a lifetime of designing rooms and being in kitchens.

Imagine the chances of a delightfully eloquent, charismatic businessman, full of life and passion, settling himself in your car and offering you the job of your dreams without you even realising it.

Index

Page numbers in **bold** refer to images.

Photography by

Tim Cooper

Other images by:

This is us

Paul O'Leary 15, 28
Robin McLellan 40

Design

Paul O'Leary 58, 59, 89
Tom Riddell 64, 65
Laura Muthesius and Nora Eisermann 82, 83,
84, 85, 98, 99, 128, 129, 130, 131, 132, 133
Zoë Parker 86, 87
Susie Brady 101
Nina Plummer 106, 107, 108, 109

Craft

Kat Major Janes 153, 163
Paul O'Leary 166, 185
Nicole Franzen 172, 173
Nina Plummer 174

Style

Helen Parker 203, 204, 205, 206, 207, 208, 209
Paul O'Leary 212, 213, 278, 279, 286, 287
Zoë Parker 230, 231, 306, 307
Max Szyrmulewicz 266

Stories

Helen Parker 320, 349, 350, 351, 352, 354
Paul O'Leary 345, 347

With thanks to Emma and Matt Macri-Waller for
the use of their beautiful deVOL kitchen on the
cover of this book.

Acknowledgements

Helen Parker

Looking through a few books and reading the acknowledgements that many authors make, it is clear that when writing a book there are so many people to thank from a single author: from their partners, family and friends to each and every person who helped bring their words to life. Our book has been written by the three of us and so the list of our acknowledgements suddenly became rather too long.

I think that reading your name with thanks in the back of a book must be a lovely sight to see and having a book dedicated to you even more of a special moment. So, it is with a little sadness for our friends and family that this list is not as personal or exhaustive as many. But there are reasons for this; the work we do is only possible because here at deVOL we have such an incredible team of people to help us and our customers and guide them through the whole kitchen experience from the moment they step into one of our showrooms.

The kitchen business is a tree with many branches, it begins with our showrooms and our showroom staff, where people get welcomed into specially created spaces in specially chosen buildings. These buildings have been carefully picked for their character, and need, in most cases, to be restored. And so, the first step begins, our little group of builders who work alongside us to make our showrooms something special. They have helped and almost rebuilt Cotes Mill in Leicestershire, St John's Square in Clerkenwell and our New York showroom on Bond Street, Manhattan, often relocating and leaving their families for months at a time to take on these lengthy projects. Their skill and work ethic is phenomenal.

We then have what began as a handful of carpenters and has now grown into an impressive workforce of joiners, painters, and general furniture builders.

Without these people we have no cupboards, no kitchens, and no business, so the workshops are really the heart of deVOL. The noise and the wood and the talent and dedication you see in the workshops makes you understand the whole meaning of manufacturing and making.

The kitchen designers are the bones of deVOL, they actually make a customer's dream become reality, they draw, and they quote, and they chat and then probably do it all over again until their customer is happy. Their knowledge, creativity and tireless hard work are what makes the whole business tick and what makes us so special as a company. Our designers work alongside our project managers, the unseen heroes of deVOL who are responsible for taking a customer's kitchen designs and turning them into a reality, they pick up and deal with all the tricky logistics and make the projects run as smoothly as they possibly can, despite or in spite of the obvious hurdles that customers and their homes face.

Then there are the packers and the pickers and the loaders and the drivers, all getting the furniture carefully and accurately signed off and ready to be taken to customers' homes. The fitters then take over and they become the face and reputation of deVOL, their skill, and quick-thinking heads, along with their charm, leave a lasting impression on all of our customers. A very immediate job that cannot afford to be done in any way other than exceptionally.

The people behind the scenes are so integral to everyone at deVOL's wellbeing and to the smooth running of the business. The details they have to understand and undertake for every single kitchen that leaves our workshop is immense. Every screw, every 10 tonnes of wood and every pot of coffee has to be thought about. Every fitter's hotel room for the night and every employee's wages paid. The ear to bend and the ear to console, the sensitivity, and the kindness and sometimes the difficult situations all must be managed and considered. There is a person for all these jobs, and they are as much part of deVOL as we are.

Our image is our trump card, it is the reason we inspire so many people around the world and what sets us apart, we take the utmost pride in every image we decide to show. Our photographer, Tim, and our Creative Design Team are behind every single image you see, every advertisement and every brochure. They turn our dreams and ideas into reality and never falter in their desire and ability to show deVOL as a truly inspirational company. They are creating the visions and scenes that go on to inspire our customers to take the next step.

Our customers were local for many years, then we found our images and style were coveted by people much further away from Leicestershire. The social media phenomenon is totally responsible for giving us a direct sign that people the world over were getting to know and love our cupboards and our photographs. The biggest following of a kitchen company in the whole world on Instagram is deVOL Kitchens, and it is all done by a very dedicated and humble team who started the journey together almost ten years ago and have tirelessly given the world a daily insight into the world of deVOL, with their eloquence and creativity. This led to us opening our Bond Street showroom in New York City and we have never looked back, as it then led to us doing two series of our show *For the Love of Kitchens* on the Magnolia Network.

The name deVOL has exponentially grown in more recent years because of our accessories, this new branch of deVOL has taken us to a much wider audience, people who may not want a kitchen. We began with Claire and Steph, in the ceramics and metal studios, respectively. Tiny little barns and sheds where they set up what is now a multi-million-pound business in interior products. They are both still here and have ever-growing teams of talented people who throw and turn and cast and fire and design our very select range of what we think are

rather special things for your home. These two people straight out of university have transformed deVOL and made it more accessible to every homemaker. As these teams grow, they need help with every aspect of running an accessories shop, so we have a very talented and growing team of product designers who ensure from concept to packaging that everything is considered. This job is at the cutting edge of deVOL and requires very creative people to take control; we are lucky enough to have a handful of such people.

Cotes Mill is our biggest showroom and where a large portion of the aforementioned people work, the industrial but beautiful building surrounded by 12 acres of land. These parts of deVOL are what makes us different: the secret garden, the wildlife, the meadows and the rivers and ponds. These grounds and buildings also need caring for and watching over day and night to protect them. We have a wonderful team of groundspeople who keep not only the inside of deVOL looking beautiful, but also the outside.

I must have missed people out and I am so sorry for this, but I think the true unsung heroes of deVOL are Paul and Robin.

Paul thought this whole deVOL thing up. Right from the start, it was him and him alone. With his reckless disregard for caution, his stupidly high levels of bravery, his inability to take the cautious option and his lack of funds, he has taken every possible opportunity to make deVOL what it is today. Definitely not the route of a faint-hearted person, this little business has grown and grown. Pure guts and raw talent, naivety and focus are why deVOL is what it is today and no other reason.

Robin is 'one of those people' who is difficult to describe without embarrassing him. His stature and blonde hair, his smart brogues and his tweed jacket are very English, and he is a true gentleman in every sense of the word. Anyone lucky enough to work with him will quickly see there is nothing (absolutely nothing) Robin can't do. He is the humble rock that keeps deVOL on track.

All rights reserved.
Published in the United States by Clarkson Potter/Publishers, an imprint
of the Crown Publishing Group, a division of Penguin Random House
LLC, New York.

Originally published in hardcover in Great Britain by Ebury Press, an
imprint of Ebury Publishing, London, in 2023.

ClarksonPotter.com

CLARKSON POTTER is a trademark and POTTER with colophon is a
registered trademark of Penguin Random House LLC.

Library of Congress Cataloging-in-Publication Data
Names: O'Leary, Paul (Director of deVOL Kitchens), author. | McLellan,
    Robin, author. | Parker, Helen (Creative director), author.
Title: The deVOL kitchen / Paul O'Leary, Robin McLellan, Helen Parker.
Description: London : Ebury Press, 2023.
Identifiers: LCCN 2023016920 (print) | LCCN 2023016921 (ebook) |
    ISBN 9780593582329 (hardcover) | ISBN 9780593582336 (ebook)
Subjects: LCSH: Kitchens. | deVOL Kitchens (Firm) | Interior decoration.
Classification: LCC NK2117.K5 O44 2023 (print) | LCC NK2117.K5
    (ebook) | DDC 747.7/97--dc23/eng/20230524
LC record available at https://lccn.loc.gov/2023016920
LC ebook record available at https://lccn.loc.gov/2023016921

ISBN 978-0-593-58232-9
Ebook ISBN 978-0-593-58233-6

Printed in China

Editor: Deanne Katz
Design: Huw Major Janes
Main photography: Tim Cooper
Additional photography: Paul O'Leary, Helen Parker, Zoë Parker, Susie
Brady, Kat Major Janes, Laura Muthesius, Nora Eisermann, Max
Szyrmulewicz, Nicole Franzen, Nina Plummer, Tom Riddell
Production manager: Heather Williamson
Marketer: Stephanie Davis

10 9 8 7 6 5 4 3 2

First Edition